BRITISH LOCOMOTIVE BUILDERS' PLATES

A PICTORIAL GUIDE

Midland Publishing Limited

BRITISH LOCOMOTIVE BUILDERS' PLATES

Keith Buckle & David Love

A PICTORIAL GUIDE

© 1994
Keith Buckle & David Love and
Midland Publishing Limited

Published by
Midland Publishing Limited
24 The Hollow, Earl Shilton
Leicester, LE9 7NA
England

ISBN 1-85780-018-4

Printed in England by
Hillman Printers (Frome) Limited
Frome, Somerset
BA11 4RW

Designed by
Midland Publishing Limited
and typeset in Swiss 721 Condensed
and Serifa Black

CONTENTS

ACKNOWLEDGEMENTS

The Authors wish to express their sincere thanks to the following for their invaluable assistance in the preparation of this book:

Clive Baines; Arnold Bimpson, Bimpson Miniature Railways; Birmingham Locomotive Club; Stewart Blencowe; Peter Briddon, Yorkshire Engine Company Limited; John Burford; Frank Burridge; Mike Charles, The Buffer Stops; the late Bruce Chennell; Alex Clark, Hunslet Barclay Limited; Robert Cooke, for his photographic expertise; Anthony Crowhurst, Crowhurst Engineering; Andy Cutcliffe; Trevor Dale; Bob Darvill; Aldo Delicata; Ron Dent; Brian Dodd; Andrew Dow; Bernard Fell, Pikrose Limited; Festiniog Railway Archives; Don Fifer, Pfeifferbahn Miniature Railways; the late Eddie Frazer; Mike Freebury; Stuart Furniss; Brian Gent, FMB Engineering Limited; Great Western Trust, Didcot; Tom Greaves, Roger Greatrex, Knightley Light Railway; the late Eric Hannan; Ivor Harding; Brian Hilton; Dave Holroyd, Narrow Gauge Railway Society; Bob Jones; Frank Jones; Wilton Jones; Patrick Keef, Alan Keef Limited; Peter Layfield; Robin Lidster; Rodney Lissenden; Trevor Lodge; John Mander, Birmingham Railway Publications; Alistair McCaig; J. McCarthy, Chief Mechanical Engineer, Inchicore Works; John Milner, Milner Engineering Chester Limited; National Railway Museum, for copyright photographs; John Palmer; Robin Patrick; David Pearson; Tony Peart, Doncaster Grammar School Museum; Richard Pelham; Peter Plater; Andy Probyn, Maxitrak Limited; The Ravenglass & Eskdale Railway Company Limited; Alan Rice; Brett Rogers, TMA Engineering Limited; Romney, Hythe & Dymchurch Light Railway; Andy Ross, The Hunslet Engine Company Ltd; Bernard Rowe; the late Richard Rutherford; Adrian Sant, Cromar White Railways; David Scudamore; Michael Severn-Lamb, Severn-Lamb Limited; Bob Shaw; Roger Shenton; Doug Sims, Ruswarp Miniature Railway; Trevor Smith; Elmer Steuernagel; Peter Tanner; Paul Tilley; George Toms; Peter Toye, Clayton Equipment Limited; Alan Whincup; Ian Wright, Sheffield Railwayana Auctions. Also, to our publishers, who have transformed our manuscript into a unique publication.

Finally, but by no means least, to our wives Joan and Patricia, for their encouragement and unfailing help with such tasks as checking the manuscript, the details of the plates and with proof reading.

Our apologies to anyone whom we may have inadvertantly forgotten.

INTRODUCTION

Of all the collectable mementos to emanate from locomotives, be they steam, diesel or electric, it could be argued that the most interesting, if only for the sheer variety, are their builders' plates. That name plates and number plates are very popular with many collectors of locomotive memorabilia is perhaps not surprising as invariably locomotives are known by their name or number and enthusiasts are conditioned to thinking in those terms. However, there is much of a sameness in style of many of those types of plate, no better example being than the pattern of name and cabside number plates perpetuated by the GWR. Inevitably a wider choice of builders' plates is available simply because only a minority of locomotives carried names and not even all were numbered but most bore some form of identification as to their origin. Builders' plates are very much a locomotive's birth certificate and in many ways their death certificate as well, as they are often all that remain of the machines that bore them. Historically, therefore, they are an important part of our railway heritage and, certainly in recent times, there has been a growing recognition of this fact, witness their current popularity at auctions.

The information given on plates regarding parentage usually comprises the manufacturer's name, the location of the workshop, date of construction and a progressive number, although there are extremes to this practice ranging from the sparse to the prolific. Perhaps the most frustrating habit is where no progressive number is quoted as it leaves no positive identification as to the locomotive from which the plate came. The most popular shapes of plate are undoubtedly oval and rectangular but others can be found such as triangular (Nasmyth Wilson), rhomboid and round (North British Locomotive Company), and hexagonal (Robert Stephenson). Their size can also vary tremendously from the diminutive as exemplified by the plates used by Ruston & Hornsby Limited of Lincoln to the simply huge such as those carried by certain of the locomotives built by Andrew Barclay Sons & Co Limited of Kilmarnock. Manufacturers have also differed in their ideas as to where to position these advertisements for their wares and whilst normally cabsides, boilers or frames of locomotives have been used, the insides of cabs and other such unlikely places have not escaped attention.

The vast majority of builders' plates are made from either brass or cast iron but more modern examples are often aluminium or even fibreglass. In the main, plates are cast with raised lettering but a number of manufacturers such as the GNR (and later the LNER) at Doncaster, Manning Wardle, Hudswell Clarke, Peckett and Kitson produced very nice engraved plates which when cleaned and polished are perhaps the most attractive of all.

The way in which progressive numbers are allocated differs from manufacturer to manufacturer although in general they are to be found in a continuous run. Sometimes, however, manufacturers whose work was not totally that of locomotive building have allocated numbers to other items of equipment they have produced, thus producing gaps in the locomotive lists. Amalgamations of firms have also complicated matters. In the case of the North British Locomotive Company for example the total output of the constituent firms of Dúbs, Neilson Reid and Sharp Stewart were added together to arrive at the number of the first product of the new company but Falcon's, predecessors of Brush of Loughborough, started an entirely new series instead of following in Hughes' footsteps. Whilst most builders commenced at number one some started at a higher figure and some, of course, as previously stated, showed no number at all. Lettering on most plates is non-serif but there are exceptions such as the large Beyer Peacock plates of the types fitted to certain of the Garratts. A few plates, such as the early Sentinels and those produced by Armstrong Whitworth, also carry logos some of which are very attractive. The subject of builders' plates is vast and varied and in this book the major manufacturers and many smaller makers have been covered. The book should not, however, be regarded as definitive. To attempt a comprehensive work would be an impossibility considering the number of locomotive builders which have existed since railways began and the variety of plates which have emanated from their workshops, the designs of which have not been recorded and are now lost forever. Although much is known about plates which have survived, new examples occasionally turn up, leaving wide open the whole field for collectors with the hope of finding something that is different. The plates in this work are all known to exist and in the main are in private collections. In a few instances, for illustrative purposes, plates still carried by locomotives or specially supplied by builders for display purposes are included. In such cases this in no way infers the availability of these plates to collectors.

The plates for each workshop are shown in order of the dates given on the plates although this may not always be the actual date of construction as builders sometimes, for various reasons, fitted plates giving incorrect information. Their dimensions are given but only to the nearest $\frac{1}{8}$" because examples of similar plates may vary very slightly in size. Details of the material from which they are made is shown. Where this is given as brass it covers bronze and gunmetal and similarly aluminium covers any plates of non-ferrous white metal.

Most plates are illustrated by means of photographs and in some instances by rubbings taken from the actual plates. Where this is not the case, a shaded background has been used to give a visual indication of the plates' shape. Superimposed on this background is the wording, on a line by line basis, in the correct sequence as on the original plate, but it is important to note that this may not necessarily match the actual layout, particularly on the oval examples where more often than not at least some of the wording will follow the curvature of the rim. Differences in the size of lettering is also omitted in these examples but the wording has been depicted correctly as serif or non-serif – the latter is known as 'sans-serif' in the graphic-arts industry. Serif lettering has a cross-line finishing off the stroke (ie T) whereas non-serif does not (ie T). Additional information relating to any particular plate is given on pages 75-76, under the heading 'Notes to the text'. The relative note is indicated by a circled number alongside the illustration.

Historical information has been derived from several sources, including *British Steam Locomotive Builders* by J.W. Lowe; *A Hunslet Hundred* by L.T.C. Rolt, and *The Springburn Story* by J. Thomas, to which further reference should be made by those wishing to know more on the subject. The publications and records of the Industrial Railway Society have also proved invaluable.

For
Joan, Angela & Iain
&
Patricia, Christopher & Timothy

PART ONE

BRITISH PRIVATE BUILDERS, AGENTS, DEALERS AND OWNERS

In this section are covered all of the well known companies with a large number of the smaller builders and a brief word is said about the firms' histories to illustrate how the railway locomotive industry in this country developed and eventually declined.

So far as the plates from the private sector are concerned it could be argued that these are by far the most interesting and varied of those produced but readers will need to judge for themselves from the illustrations. These builders between them produced many locomotives for export and some of the older and rarer plates depicted owe their existence to this enterprise as often ancient work horses soldiered on abroad long after their counterparts had gone to the scrap heap over here, well before collecting became fashionable. The survival of these plates is in a way, as is that of all plates, a tribute to their builders.

In more recent times many of those private builders who had survived all other obstacles finally went to the wall either through contracting markets, the prevailing economy or because they simply failed to adapt enough, or at all, to fight off foreign competition for the supply of diesel and electric traction for the world's railways. The result is that today those firms which now remain in the loco-motive building industry are comparatively few and far between.

The story of builders' plates in the private sector is complex and becomes even more so if account is taken of replacement or addi-tional plates giving construction details or dates which were fitted by agents, dealers, owners or those firms that rebuilt locomotives. Although these must be regarded as cousins to builders' plates they are often of interest to collectors of such items and therefore warrant some coverage.

During their term of trading many firms have changed their title to greater or lesser degrees. In this section the firms are listed under what is in the view of the authors their most well known name. For example, Hudswell & Clarke, Hudswell Clarke & Rodgers, Hudswell Clarke & Company and Hudswell Badger can all be found under

Hudswell Clarke & Company Limited. However, where the change of name is completely different as in the case, for example, when Peckett & Sons acquired Fox Walker & Company's business, the companies are shown under separate headings. It should be noted that because of the format used in the book and the wish to include as much as possible within the constraints of the space available, it was not always possible to list the builders in this section of the work in strict alphabetical order, although they will be found under the appropriate letter of the alphabet albeit slightly out of sequence. Any problems can easily be resolved by reference to the index.

Photograph on this page courtesy of The Hunslet Engine Co Ltd.

ALLAN ANDREWS & COMPANY

Britannia Works, Kilmarnock

From 1873 to the time of closure in 1884 the Britannia Works undertook locomotive building variously under the titles of Allan Andrews & Company, Andrews Barr & Company and Barr Morrison & Company. About 30 or so locomotives were constructed; these appear to have been allocated progressive numbers in a straight run starting at one.

Raised   Brass   10" x 6⅛"

ATKINSON-WALKER WAGONS LIMITED

Frenchwood Works, Preston

This Company produced locomotives for only five years between 1926 and 1930, all of which were vertical boiler machines. It is believed that in total their maximum output was no greater than 25.

Raised   Brass   9" diameter

SIR W. G. ARMSTRONG WHITWORTH & CO LTD

Scotswood Works, Newcastle-on-Tyne

Although Armstrong Whitworth produced locomotives during two periods in the nineteenth century, their main entry into this field was not until after the First World War, when their shell factories at Scotswood were converted for the construction of locomotives. The first of these was turned out in 1919 and production continued until 1937. In spite of the operation lasting for less than 20 years, over 1400 locomotives were built and Armstrong Whitworth's products were exported far and wide, to such destinations as Argentina, Australia, Egypt, Indonesia, and Nigeria.

In the main, Armstrong Whitworth used rectangular builders' plates but in some cases oval varieties were produced. Most carried the companies emblem, originally a monogram of AW and later an arm holding an hammer. A separate series of progressive numbers was used for diesel production; these were prefixed by the letter D.

Raised   Brass   5⅞" x 3⅞"

Raised   Brass   14½" x 8½"

Raised   Brass   5¾" x 3⅞"

Raised   Brass   12" x 7"

Raised   Brass   5¾" x 3⅞"

Raised   Brass   18" x 12"

Raised   Brass   8⅛" x 5"

Raised   Brass   8" x 4⅞"

Raised   Brass   8" x 4¾"

Raised   Brass   8¼" x 5"

ASSOCIATED ELECTRICAL INDUSTRIES LIMITED

Manchester

Associated Electrical Industries Limited was formed in 1928 as a holding company controlling The British Thomson-Houston Company Limited and Metropolitan-Vickers Electrical Company Limited, both of which continued to trade under their separate names until 1958, when they became AEI (Rugby) and AEI (Manchester) respectively. The firm became part of GEC in 1967.

Engraved Aluminium 5" x 1 5/8"

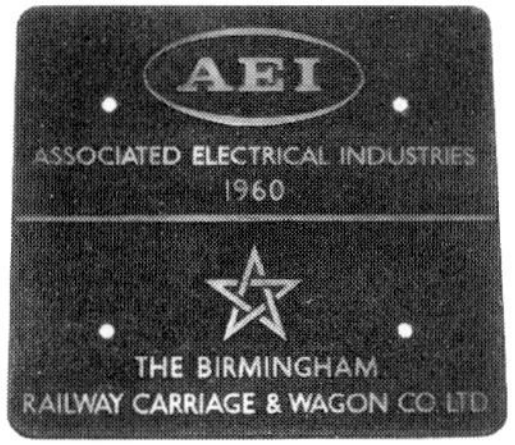

Raised Brass 13" x 11 1/2"

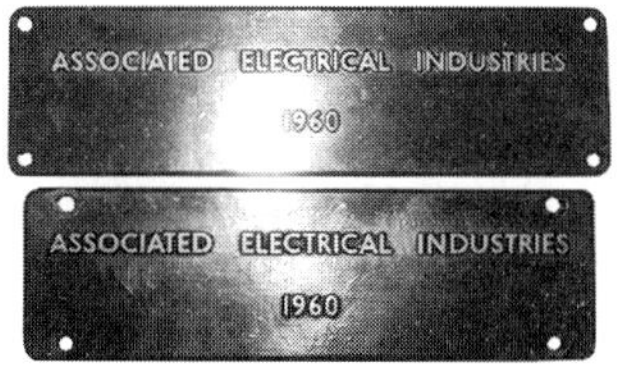

Raised Aluminium 18"/17" x 5"

AVONSIDE ENGINE COMPANY LIMITED

Bristol

Henry Stothert & Company (later Stothert, Slaughter & Company) set up business in 1837 in Avon Street, St. Philips, and in 1864 changed their title to the Avonside Engine Company. Initially the firm concentrated on building main line locomotives, but eventually decided to devote themselves to constructing smaller types, as their existing workshops were unable to cope. This policy was introduced in 1881 and continued until the firm's closure. It was brought about mainly because of financial reasons following the death of Edward Slaughter and the liquidation of the old Avonside Company. A new concern of the same name was formed to carry on work in the old premises, but in 1905 the business moved to new works at Fishponds. They were, however, unable to weather the recession between the two World Wars and went into voluntary liquidation at the end of 1934.

Until just before the First World War a large oval plate was in use, but from then onwards a smaller oval became standard. Several variations of both types are known. Some of these were decorated with a star each side of the word Bristol.

Raised Brass 14 1/4" x 8 1/4"

Raised Brass 14" x 8 3/8"

(42)

Raised Brass 14 1/8" x 8"

(64)

Raised Brass 14 1/8" x 8"

Raised Brass 10 3/4" x 6 1/2"

Raised Brass 10 7/8" x 6 1/2"

Raised Brass 10 1/4" x 6 3/8"

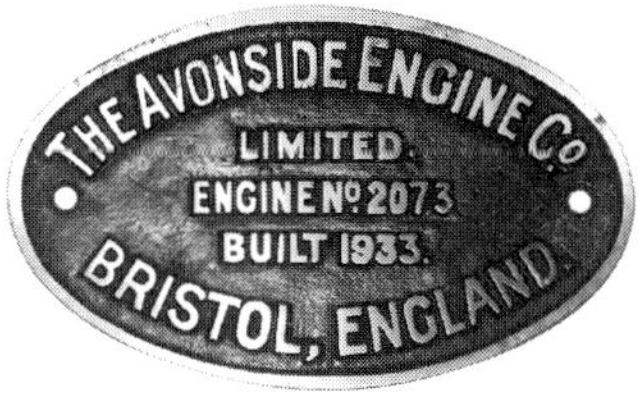

Raised Brass 12 1/4" x 7 3/8"

AVELING & PORTER LIMITED

Invicta Works, Rochester

Thomas Aveling founded his business in 1850 and produced his first road traction engine in 1861. Richard Porter became his partner in the following year and in 1864 the first traction engine for use on rails was constructed. Approximately 130 of these machines were built, the last leaving the works in early 1926. All were 4-wheeled locomotives and ranged from 4 to 20 hp.

Engraved Brass 10 1/4" x 7 1/2"

Raised   Brass   8" x 5½"

E. E. BAGULEY LIMITED
Burton-on-Trent

In 1911 this concern began trading in the former Rykneild lorry works in Burton-on-Trent under the title Baguley (Cars) Limited, producing inspection cars, railcars, locomotives and rolling stock for the railway market. The name changed to Baguley (Engineers) Limited in 1920, and during that decade 31 steam locomotives were built. They traded until fairly recent times, latterly as Baguley-Drewry Limited.

Raised   Brass   5½" x 3½"

BAGULEY [ENGINEERS] L^TD
No: 2042
1931
BURTON on TRENT

Engraved   Brass   4" x 2½"

W. G. BAGNALL
LIMITED
Castle Engine Works, Stafford

W. G. Bagnall Limited was set up comparatively late (1875) in the field of locomotive building by William Gordon Bagnall and at first dealt with all kinds of machinery. The first locomotive was built in 1876 and carried the works number 16, a good example of the practice which some firms adopted of allocating such identification to products other than locomotives. Bagnall's however rectified this state of affairs in 1893 and from then on consecutive numbers were used. The firm became a Limited Company in 1887 and, having managed to survive two World Wars and the depression, became Brush-Bagnall Traction Ltd in 1951. After several other changes of ownership the works was taken over by the English Electric Company in 1961, and, as a result of a policy decision by the new owners to transfer all locomotive work to their plants at Darlington and Newton-le-Willows, the last locomotive, works No.3208, which was a 4wDH, left the shops in November of that year.

Raised   Cast Iron   13⅞" x 9"

Raised   Brass   6½" x 4¼"

W. G. BAGNALL L^TD
N° 2221
1927
STAFFORD, ENGLAND

Raised   Brass   6" x 4"

Raised   Brass   6⅜" x 4¼"

Raised   Brass   13¾" x 7¾"

Raised   Brass   13¾" x 7¾"

Raised   Brass   11⅞" x 7"

Raised   Brass   8" x 5⅜"

Raised   Brass   6¼" x 4¼"

Raised   Brass   4½" x 2½"

ANDREW BARCLAY SONS & COMPANY LIMITED

Caledonia Works, Kilmarnock

This company produced its first locomotive in 1859, and is today one of the few concerns that have survived out of the once numerous firms which manufactured locomotives in the Kilmarnock area. It is now known as Hunslet Barclay Limited. Not surprisingly, during its existence, the firm, which has mainly produced locomotives for the industrial market, has used various styles of plate. Early examples seem to have comprised both rectangular and oval types. These eventually evolved into a large and impressive rectangular pattern which was used from the late 1880s to the mid-1890s, before being superseded by the equally impressive but better known large oval which, with some exceptions, became standard until after the Second World War. A smaller oval pattern was then introduced which has continued in use until the present day, but now bears the Hunslet Barclay name. A separate series of progressive numbers was used for steam and diesel production.

Raised   Brass   8⅝" x 4¼"

Raised   Brass   9½" x 6⅛"

Raised   Brass   16⅞" x 7½"

Raised   Brass   17" x 7½"

Raised   Brass   18½" x 7⅝"

①

Raised   Brass   9⅜" x 7"

Raised   Brass   16¾" x 11¾"

Raised   Brass   16" x 9"

②
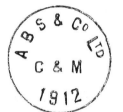

Raised   Brass   7" diameter

Raised   Brass   9¾" x 7¼"

Raised   Brass   8⅞" x 5¾"

③
④

Raised   Brass   16¾" x 11¾"

Raised   Brass   9⅞" x 7"

Raised   Brass   16¾" x 11⅝"

Raised   Brass   9¹/₈" x 6³/₄"

Raised   Aluminium   9³/₄" x 7¹/₄"

Raised   Aluminium   9³/₄" x 7¹/₄"

Raised   Aluminium   9⁷/₈" x 7⁷/₈"

Raised   Cast Iron   10" x 7¹/₈"

BARCLAYS
& COMPANY

River Bank Engine Works, Kilmarnock

This firm should not be confused with Andrew Barclay and Sons, although it was very closely linked with that concern, being a direct off-shoot set up by Andrew Barclay in 1872 for his sons and brother. It is possible that the idea was to transfer the locomotive side of his business here and let Caledonia Works concentrate on producing mining equipment. Whatever the plan was, the new business lasted sixteen years before being sold and all the work returning to Caledonia Works.

At that stage the series of progressive numbers used by both concerns were added together, causing Andrew Barclay's to jump from 311 to 636. This was, however, exaggerated, as Barclays & Company's numbers commenced at either 200 or 201 and finished in the low 300s.

Raised   Brass   10³/₄" x 6⁷/₈"

ALBERT BARNES & CO
Albion Works, Rhyl

Albion Works built six 4-4-2 Atlantic type locomotives between 1920 and 1934, five being for the Rhyl Marine Lake Miniature Railway, where Mr Albert Barnes was the Manager, and one for the Margate Dreamland Miniature Railway. All locomotives were of 15" gauge.

The plate depicted is from a locomotive originally built by W. J. Bassett Lowke Limited, of Northampton, and is thought to be an Albert Barnes repair or rebuild plate.

Engraved   Brass   4³/₄" x 3³/₈"

BELL BROS
LIMITED
Port Clarence

In 1907 Bell Bros Limited carried out a rebuild of a Black Hawthorn 0-4-0ST and fitted the plate shown below. The claim that they actually built this machine is, therefore, spurious. Bell Bros became part of Dorman Long & Company Limited in May 1923.

Raised   Brass   10⁵/₈" x 4⁷/₈"

BASS, RATCLIFF
& GRETTON LIMITED
Burton-on-Trent

The Bass brewery railway at Burton-on-Trent was famed for its fleet of immaculate 0-4-0STs. They were handsome machines built mainly by a local firm, Thornewill & Warham Ltd and Neilson Reid & Co of Glasgow. Conventional builders' plates were, however, disregarded in favour of large engraved plates giving the firm's name, the date of the locomotive's construction and depicting the Bass red triangle.

Engraved   Brass   15¹/₂" x 9¹/₄"

Engraved   Brass   15¹/₂" x 9¹/₄"

WILLIAM BEARDMORE & COMPANY LIMITED

Dalmuir Works, Glasgow

This company had its origins in the early days of ship-building on the Clyde, when, in 1835, Robert Napier acquired a forge at Parkhead. The business subsequently passed to the Beardmore family, and in 1886 William Beardmore Junior took charge. Many kinds of work were undertaken, including general engineering, ships, weapons, automobiles and aircraft. In 1900 the factory at Dalmuir was acquired and after the First World War these premises were converted to build locomotives, whilst those at Parkhead undertook repairs and rebuildings, though Dalmuir did share in this activity when work was slack between orders. The first new locomotive was completed in 1920 and was given progressive No.100. When production ceased in 1931, 395 units had been built and of these 220 went to railways in this country and all but four were steam.

Beardmore plates appear to have been of two distinct and unusual patterns. Locomotive building at Dalmuir fell into two periods from 1920 to 1924 and from 1927 to 1931 and during the first of these it seems that the rhomboid version was used throughout. During the second period, a rectangular plate was introduced although the rhomboid plate was applied to some locomotives.

Raised   Brass   8½" x 3¾"

Raised   Brass   7⅝" x 4½"

BEYER, PEACOCK & COMPANY LIMITED

Gorton Foundry, Manchester

In 1854 Charles Beyer and Richard Peacock set up their business in Gorton, Manchester, and the following year produced their first locomotive, a standard gauge 2-2-2 for the Great Western Railway. They soon built up a first class reputation for good workmanship and in only a little over 50 years had produced their 5000th locomotive. The types built at Gorton were extremely varied and were exported world-wide. Some industrial locomotives were built, but the major part of production was for main line railways.

Many notable locomotives were produced but none more so than the Beyer-Garratts, with which the firm's name became synonymous. With encroachment of diesel traction, both at home and overseas, Beyer Peacock tried to move with the times and in 1961 reorganised to meet the new challenge. Unfortunately they chose to back diesel locomotives with hydraulic transmission whereas British Railways decided that its future requirements should be based on diesel electric locomotives. Sufficient orders were not forthcoming, so the company went into voluntary liquidation and by 1966 the works were being dismantled.

The variety of plates used by Beyer Peacock is truly amazing and no other British Company can match the number of variations, at least seventy being known. These comprise a number of different sized ovals, half-moon splasher plates, full size splasher plates akin to nameplates, and rectangular plates.

Raised   Brass   14⅝" x 6¾"

Raised   Brass   21⅛" x 4½"

Raised   Brass   14½" x 6¾"

Raised   Brass   27⅝" x 5⅛"

Raised   Brass   21⅛" x 10¾"

BEYER PEACOCK & Cº LTD
MANCHESTER 1887.

Raised   Brass   17¼" x 3⅞"

Raised   Brass   15⅜" x 3⅜"

BEYER, PEACOCK & Cº LTD
1887
MANCHESTER.

Raised   Brass   26" x 5¼"

Raised   Brass   16¾" x 7⅞"

Raised   Brass $63^{5}/_{8}"$ x 6"

Raised   Brass $17^{3}/_{4}"$ x $8^{3}/_{8}"$

Raised   Brass $9^{5}/_{8}"$ x $5^{5}/_{8}"$

Raised   Brass   17" x 8"

Raised   Brass $9^{3}/_{4}"$ x $5^{5}/_{8}"$

Raised   Brass $18^{7}/_{8}"$ x $9^{5}/_{8}"$

Raised   Brass $18^{3}/_{4}"$ x $9^{1}/_{4}"$

Raised   Brass $6^{5}/_{8}"$ x $4^{3}/_{8}"$

⑥⑤

Raised   Brass $11^{1}/_{2}"$ x $6^{3}/_{4}"$

Raised   Brass $18^{5}/_{8}"$ x $9^{1}/_{2}"$

Raised   Brass $17^{7}/_{8}"$ x $8^{1}/_{2}"$

Raised   Brass $9^{7}/_{8}"$ x $4^{3}/_{4}"$

Raised   Brass $9^{7}/_{8}"$ x $5^{3}/_{4}"$

Raised   Brass   18" x $8^{1}/_{2}"$

Raised   Brass   18" x $8^{5}/_{8}"$

Raised   Brass   10" x 5³/₄"

Raised   Brass   10" x 5⁷/₈"

Raised   Brass   13⁵/₈" x 6⁵/₈"

Raised   Brass   13⁵/₈" x 6¹/₂"

Raised   Brass   10" x 5³/₄"

Raised   Brass   18⁷/₈" x 9³/₄"

Raised   Brass   19" x 9³/₄"

Raised   Brass   13¹/₂" x 6¹/₂"

(5)

Raised   Brass   13¹/₂" x 7¹/₂"

Raised   Brass   10³/₈" x 6³/₈"

Raised   Brass   14¹/₄" x 7¹/₈"

Raised   Brass   10" x 5"

(6)

Raised   Brass   10¹/₈" x 5³/₄"

Raised   Brass   18⁷/₈" x 9⁵/₈"

Raised   Brass   13⁵/₈" x 6¹/₂"

(7)

Raised   Brass   10¹/₂" x 6³/₈"

Raised   Brass   13¾" x 6¾"

Raised   Brass   13⅝" x 6⅝"

Raised   Brass   13⅝" x 6⅝"

Raised   Brass   10½" x 6½"

Raised   Aluminium   12¾" x 5⅛"

Raised   Aluminium   12⅛" x 5⅛"

Raised   Aluminium   8⅞" x 3⅜"

Raised   Aluminium   13⅛" x 6½"

BIMPSON MINIATURE RAILWAYS
Maghull

The beginnings of Arnold Bimpson's interest in building miniature locomotives dates back to 1950, but it was not until 1979 that regular production began with the construction of a 7¼" gauge petrol hydrostatic locomotive for the Halton Miniature Railway Society. This machine bore a small oval aluminium plate inscribed 'A. BIMPSON MAGHULL LOCO WORKS' and later these plates were also used on rolling stock. In 1983, now operating as Bimpson Miniature Engineering, a larger oval plate was introduced. In the mid 1980s Mr Bimpson ceased trading due to health reasons, but then recommenced his hobby and on later locomotives, plates with the title 'BIMPSON MINIATURE RAILWAYS' were used. Some of these had the word LOCO and the number and date cast in.

The locomotives produced in the early years ranged from 3½" to 7¼" gauge, but since 1979 all have been of 7¼" gauge, with one exception, that being a complete rebuild of a 10¼" gauge locomotive which was originally a Triang Minic electric. By mid 1993 a total of twenty-six locomotives had been constructed including several steam. Progressive numbers were first introduced in 1982 beginning at 6, and by mid 1993 had reached 25, although it should be noted that nine locomotives had been completed before that date and that there is no number 8 or 9, probably due to a frustrated order, or number 13.

⑧

Raised   Aluminium   3⅝" x 2⅜"

⑧

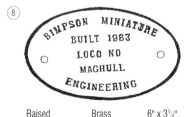

Raised   Brass   6" x 3⅝"

⑧

Raised   Brass   6⅛" x 3⅝"

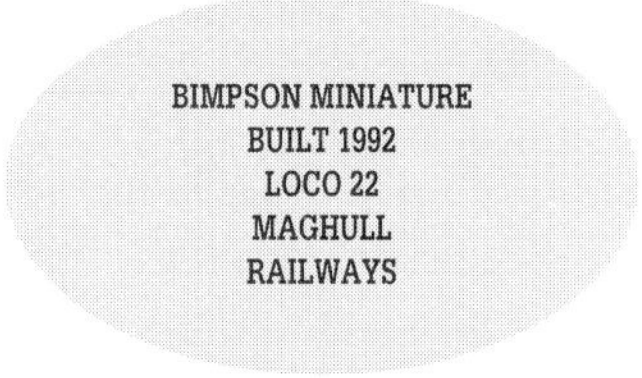

BIMPSON MINIATURE
BUILT 1992
LOCO 22
MAGHULL
RAILWAYS

Raised   Brass   6⅛" x 3⅝"

E. BORROWS & SONS
Providence Works, St. Helens

Borrows were general engineers, and, so far as railway locomotives were concerned, built only 0-4-0WTs. They were unusual machines, somewhat reminiscent of old toy wind-up trains, but nevertheless quite pleasing in appearance. Building took place between 1875 and 1910 and around 40 locomotives were constructed. H. W. Johnson & Company subsequently took over this work and built three more between 1913 and 1921.

Raised   Brass   15⅛" x 9"

THE BIRMINGHAM RAILWAY CARRIAGE & WAGON CO LTD

Smethwick Works, Smethwick

Birmingham Wagon Co Ltd was registered in March 1855, and carried on a business as dealers in selling and hiring wagons to various railway companies. About 1866 workshops were built near to the GWR Handsworth and Smethwick station, where they commenced building wagons for their hiring and selling business. In November 1878 the company name was changed to The Birmingham Railway Carriage & Wagon Co Ltd and eventually they became involved in the manufacture of all types of rolling stock including railcars and diesel and electric locomotives. The works closed in September 1963 and the area is now a trading estate.

| Raised | Brass/Chromed | 8" x 3¾" |

⑨

| Raised | Brass | 4" x 3" |

⑨

| Raised | Brass | 4" x 3" |

⑩

| Raised | Brass/Chromed | 8" x 5¾" |

BLACK, HAWTHORN & COMPANY

Gateshead-on-Tyne

When, in 1865, the firm of R. Coulthard & Company ceased to trade, its business was taken over by William Black and Thomas Hawthorn under the rather sinister sounding title of Black, Hawthorn & Company. Coulthard's had built about twenty locomotives over the period from 1834 and the new partnership developed this business, so much so that during the thirty-one years when they traded, around 1100 were turned out. Most of these were for industrial users, although a few tender locomotives were also constructed. In 1896 the firm was purchased by Chapman & Furneaux.

Black Hawthorn appear to have originally used engraved oval plates but these were eventually superseded by brass ovals with raised lettering, of which several different patterns are known.

| Engraved | Brass | 10" x 6" |

| Raised | Brass | 11½" x 7⅝" |

| Raised | Brass | 13⅞" x 9¼" |

BLACK, HAWTHORN & Cº
Nº 696
ENGINEERS
1883
GATESHEAD ON TYNE

| Raised | Brass | 15½" x 10" |

BLACK, HAWTHORN & Cº
Nº 859
ENGINEERS
1885
GATESHEAD ON TYNE

| Raised | Brass | 12½" x 7" |

| Raised | Brass | 8½" x 5" |

| Raised | Brass | 15⅝" x 10⅛" |

| Raised | Brass | 15⅞" x 10" |

BRASSEY & COMPANY
Canada Works, Birkenhead

For a little over twenty years from the mid 1850s this firm produced locomotives. Well over two hundred were built, the majority going for export.

| Raised | Cast Iron | 13⁵/₈" x 5¼" |

BRITISH DYESTUFFS CORPORATION LTD
Huddersfield

Private operators of locomotives were usually able to carry out minor repair work at their own premises sometimes in primitive conditions. Presumably BDC must have had adequate workshop facilities to undertake the rebuilding of a locomotive as the plate illustrated states. The engine was an Andrew Barclay of 1918 vintage. British Dyestuffs later became part of the ICI empire.

| Raised | Brass | 7⁷/₈" x 5" |

THE BRUSH ELECTRICAL ENGINEERING CO LTD
Falcon Works, Loughborough

In 1889 the Anglo-American Brush Electric Light Corporation acquired the Falcon Railway Plant Works and formed The Brush Electrical Engineering Company. Locomotive building continued although no further steam locomotives were constructed after 1914. The firm entered the diesel market just before the Second World War, when they converted their works shunter, an 0-4-0ST, but it was not until the beginning of the 1950s that this business became a major factor, when Brush became associated with W. G. Bagnall Limited of Stafford and Brush-Bagnall Traction Limited was formed, specifically to compete in this field. This partnership lasted only until January 1956, when the two firms again went their separate ways and Brush Traction was born. The firm's reputation has grown steadily since then.

On its steam locomotives, Brush continued to use a plate based on that of its predecessors, but after a few years replaced it by a larger oval. When diesel construction began in earnest in the 1950s under Brush-Bagnall an oval plate lettered 'Brush / Bagnall / No.XXXX / 19XX / Loughborough England' was introduced. The progressive numbers shown on these plates were within the series used by Bagnalls. On the break-up of the partnership Brush Traction continued to used the same style of plate but commenced a new series of progressive numbers starting at No.71, by referring back to the diesels that had previously been built at Falcon Works. 'Kestrel' broke with the tradition of the oval plate and was fitted with a rectangular engraved plate in aluminium. This became the norm and British Rail's Class 60s have, for example, been fitted with two attractive versions of these.

| Raised | Brass | 15³/₄" x 9³/₄" |

| Raised | Brass | 7" x 5" |

| Raised | Brass | 9³/₄" x 5³/₄" |

(61)

| Raised | Aluminium | 9⁵/₈" x 5³/₄" |

| Raised | Aluminium | 9¼" x 5⁵/₈" |

| Printed | Aluminium | 10³/₄" x 7¹/₈" |

| Engraved | Aluminium | 8" x 3¹/₂" |

| Engraved | Aluminium | Not known |

Raised/Engraved   Aluminium   9³/₄" x 5³/₄"

Raised/Engraved   Aluminium   9³/₄" x 5³/₄"

THE BRITISH THOMSON-HOUSTON CO LTD
Rugby

The British Thomson-Houston Company Limited, a subsidiary of American Thomson Houston, was established in 1896, and combined with Metropolitan-Vickers Electrical Company Limited to form Associated Electrical Industries Limited in 1928. Until 1958, however, it continued to trade under its own name.

Raised   Brass   10⁷/₈" x 6¹/₈"

CHAPMAN & FURNEAUX
Gateshead-on-Tyne

This firm were the successors to Black Hawthorn & Company Limited but traded only for a comparatively short period between 1896 and 1902, producing during that time industrial tank locomotives. They continued to use the Black Hawthorn series of progressive numbers.

Raised   Brass   11¹/₂" x 7⁵/₈"

Raised   Brass   12" x 7⁷/₈"

THE CLAYTON EQUIPMENT COMPANY LIMITED
Record Works, Hatton, Derby

The company was founded in 1931 by Mr S. R. Devlin to manufacture locomotives and railcars and as general engineers. Under his direction the firm prospered and in 1946 acquired the premises known as Record Works at Hatton. Many types of locomotives, together with other equipment, were produced both for the home market and overseas.

In 1957 International Combustion (Holdings) Limited acquired the whole of the shareholding in the company but nevertheless it continued to operate on a self contained basis. This proved to be a valuable alliance when the Class 17 Bo-Bo Diesel Electrics were produced for British Railways between 1962 and 1964 as part of the modernisation plan. Inadequate production capacity at Hatton, partly due to the success of the company in breaking into the Canadian market with their mining locomotives, was compensated for by the renting of a manufacturing area at International Combustion's premises in Derby.

In more recent times International Combustion were acquired by Clarke Chapman Limited of Gateshead chiefly because of their boiler expertise. Clarke Chapman then merged with Reyrolle Parsons to form Northern Engineering Industries and in 1989 NEI became a Rolls-Royce company.

Raised   Aluminium   7¹/₂" x 3³/₄"

Raised   Aluminium   7¹/₂" x 3³/₄"

Raised   Brass   8" x 3³/₄"

Raised   Brass   8¹/₈" x 3³/₄"

Engraved   Aluminium   9¹/₄" x 3¹/₈"

CLAYTON WAGONS LIMITED
Abbey Works, Lincoln

This company was an off-shoot of Clayton Shuttleworth & Company and between the end of the First World War and the late 1920s built a number of four-wheeled vertical boilered locomotives and railcars for both home and overseas railways.

Raised   Brass   4¼" x 6½"

CROWHURST ENGINEERING
Hythe

Anthony Crowhurst founded the firm in June 1983 although before that he had worked part time. The firm are general engineers and the style of plate shown is used on their larger products. Their locomotives and larger contracts have order numbers which are allocated from the same series and by mid 1993 had reached around 1500. At that time three diesel and two steam locomotives had been constructed as complete units, the largest being 10¼" gauge.

⑧

Raised   Brass   4½" x 2¾"

CONSETT IRON COMPANY LIMITED
Consett

This company had a large fleet of locomotives and undertook major repair and rebuilding work in their Templetown workshops. Two 0-6-0 diesel locomotives were also constructed, one in 1956 and the other in 1958. The plate illustrated is from a locomotive rebuilt at Templetown workshops. This comprised parts from an Andrew Barclay saddle tank of 1940 and a 1937 built R. & W. Hawthorn Leslie saddle tank which had itself been rebuilt by the Consett Iron Company Limited in 1951, from parts donated by a Robert Stephenson & Hawthorns saddle tank built in 1941.

Engraved   Brass   9½" x 5⅝"

COWLISHAW WALKER ENGINEERING CO LTD
Biddulph, Stoke-on-Trent

From about 1930 this company was involved in producing machinery for the mining industry and occupied the workshops of the former Norton & Biddulph Collieries Limited, and over the next few years rebuilt many of the collieries locomotives. The plate shown was from a locomotive originally built by Black, Hawthorn & Company in 1888, rebuilt by Robert Heath & Sons Limited, (who until about 1920 were the previous owners of the colliery) in 1902 and 1914. The locomotive was rebuilt again in 1932 by Cowlishaw Walker Engineering Company Limited.

Raised   Cast Iron   16¾" x 9⅞"

CROMAR WHITE LIMITED
Ringwood

Founded in 1946, Cromar White Limited manufactured a varied selection of products ranging from 4 wheel agricultural tractors, all types of commercial vehicle bodies, flight simulators for pilot training and thousands of stacking trays for a jam factory.

The miniature railway side of the business started up in 1964 and has included the building of many complete miniature railways in addition to fulfilling orders for individual locomotives. Most of the locomotives built to date have been of 7¼" gauge, but a few of 9½" and 10¼" gauge have also been built. With one exception all locomotives have been non steam, the exception being a steam railcar built in the 1970s, which was based on the R. & W. Hawthorn, Leslie's design of steam railmotor built for the Port Talbot Railway & Dock Company in 1906.

⑧

Printed   Brass   2½" x 1½"

DAVEY, PAXMAN & COMPANY LIMITED
Standard Ironworks, Colchester

Davey, Paxman & Company Limited, were general engineers, but built a small number of steam locomotives and traction engines.

Their first locomotive, built in 1922-23 was for the Ravenglass & Eskdale Railway in Cumberland, and was the first 2-8-2 on any British railway.

Apart from one or two stationary engines the only other locomotives built by the firm were the seven engines for the 15" gauge Romney, Hythe & Dymchurch Railway in Kent, between 1925 and 1927. All of these fine machines still operate today.

| Raised | Brass | 6½" x 3¾" |

DE WINTON & COMPANY
Union Iron Works, Carnarvon

Founded in the 1840s this company manufactured various equipment such as mining machinery and stationary and marine engines. Between about 1867 and the late 1890s approximately sixty vertical-boiled locomotives were built, all of which were of narrow gauge.

| Engraved | Brass | 6⅞" x 3⅞" |

DICK, KERR & CO LTD
Britannia Engineering Works, Kilmarnock

Perhaps better known for its association with the supply of tramway equipment, this firm did, however, produce a number of steam locomotives between 1883 and 1918. Following the sale of the works to The Kilmarnock Engineering Company Limited in 1919, all work was transferred to their factory at Preston and no further steam locomotives were built.

| Raised | Brass | 9½" x 6" |

| Raised | Brass | 9¼" x 6" |

THE DREWRY CAR COMPANY LIMITED
London

From its inception in 1906 to the time it went into voluntary liquidation in 1970, The Drewry Car Co had the distinction of never having actually built a locomotive itself, and throughout its existence acted solely as a sales organization. All its products were built under sub-contract by such firms as E. E. Baguley at Burton-on-Trent, English Electric at Preston, The Vulcan Foundry at Newton-le-Willows and Robert Stephenson & Hawthorns at Darlington and Newcastle-upon-Tyne.

| Raised | Brass | 7" x 4½" |

⑪

| Raised | Brass | 8⅛" x 4½" |

| Raised | Brass | 8¼" x 4½" |

| Raised | Brass | 8¼" x 4½" |

⑫

| Raised | Brass | 8" x 5" |

| Raised | Brass | 8" x 5" |

Raised   Brass   8" x 5"

Raised   Brass   8" x 5"

Raised   Brass   8" x 5"

Raised   Brass   8" x 5"

Raised   Brass   8" x 5"

(13)

Raised   Brass   8" x 5"

Raised   Brass   8" x 5"

DÚBS & COMPANY
Locomotive Works, Glasgow

In 1863 Henry Dúbs who was a partner with Neilson & Company, decided to set up his own company and in April 1864 a start was made on building a factory in what is now the Polmadie area of Glasgow. To his credit Dúbs was very successful with his enterprise as, within twelve months of the first sod being turned, the factory was in full production. Locomotives were supplied to overseas railways and to the home market and up to the merger of 1903, when the North British Locomotive Company Limited was formed, a total of 4485 were produced.

When Glasgow Locomotive Works was erected, the clay which came from the site works was used to make the bricks for the building and these were stamped with the diamond shape which became famous as the firm's trade mark. This was perpetuated in the shape of the builders' plates used on their locomotives, and the same style was continued by the North British Locomotive Company until the end of their existence in 1962.

Raised   Brass   13$^{7}/_{16}$" x 5$^{1}/_{2}$"

Raised   Brass   Not known

Raised   Brass   12$^{1}/_{2}$" x 5$^{1}/_{2}$"

Raised   Brass   13$^{1}/_{2}$" x 5$^{1}/_{2}$"

EARL OF DUDLEY
Round Oak Works, Castle Mill, Dudley

One or more narrow gauge locomotives appear to have been built in the late 19th Century and these were followed by two standard gauge 0-6-0 STs in 1912 and 1915. A number of extensive rebuilds were also undertaken. The plate illustrated is from a standard gauge 0-4-0 tender locomotive.

Engraved   Brass   24$^{1}/_{4}$" x 6$^{1}/_{4}$"

EBBW VALE STEEL IRON & COAL CO LTD

In twelve years from 1905 this firm built eight locomotives, some from kits supplied by Peckett & Sons of Bristol. In addition locomotives were also rebuilt at the Ebbw Vale workshops.

Engraved Brass 12⁷/₈" x 8"

Raised Brass 8" x 6"

THE ENGLISH ELECTRIC COMPANY LIMITED
Dick Kerr Works, Preston
Stephenson Works, Darlington
Vulcan Works, Newton-le-Willows

In 1919 the English Electric Company Limited was created after the merger of several firms and commenced locomotive construction in the former Dick Kerr Works at Preston. In the 1930s many of their products were constructed in association with The Drewry Car Company Limited. During the 1950s locomotive production was switched away from Preston mainly to The Vulcan Foundry Limited at Newton-le-Willows and Robert Stephenson & Hawthorns Limited, at Darlington, and in 1962 both of these companies came under full English Electric control. In 1964, however, Darlington was closed and building work was concentrated at Newton-le-Willows. In 1967 and 1968 respectively Associated Electrical Industries and English Electric were acquired by the General Electric Company Limited and a few locomotives were later produced with AEI/ENGLISH ELECTRIC plates. By 1972, however, plates bearing the wording GEC TRACTION LTD appeared.

This company used a standard rectangular plate of very similar design throughout its existance, but there were certain exceptions as with many firms. Perhaps one of the most unusual of those known are the round Cory, Wright & Salmon sub-contractor plates fitted to certain electric locomotives that worked on the New Zealand Government Railways.

The firm's progressive numbers were the subject of arithmetical exercises in later years and these have resulted in quite an array. Many plates carried by locomotives built at Darlington and Newton-le-Willows also show the Robert Stephenson & Hawthorns and Vulcan Foundry progressive numbers. Some plates also carry the English Electric motif of two entwined Es in a circle.

Raised Brass 10¼" x 4½"

Raised Brass 11³/₈" diameter

Raised Brass 17³/₄" x 13"

Raised Brass/Chromed 10¹/₈" x 4³/₈"

Raised Brass 10" x 4³/₈"

Raised Brass 16⁷/₈" x 10³/₈"

Raised Brass 16⁷/₈" x 10½"

Raised Brass 9⁷/₈" x 4³/₈"

Raised Brass/Chromed 10¹/₈" x 4³/₈"

Raised Brass/Chromed 10" x 4³/₈"

Raised Brass/Chromed 12¹/₂" x 7"

Raised Brass/Chromed 10¹/₈" x 4¹/₂"

Raised Brass 10¹/₈" x 4¹/₂"

⑭

Raised Brass 10" x 4³/₈"

Raised Brass/Chromed 10¹/₈" x 4¹/₂"

Raised Brass/Chromed 10¹/₈" x 4¹/₂"

⑮

Raised Aluminium 8¹/₂" x 6¹/₂"

Raised Brass 10¹/₄" x 4¹/₂"

Raised Brass 10¹/₄" x 4⁵/₈"

GEORGE ENGLAND & CO
Hatcham Ironworks, New Cross, London

In 1849, approximately ten years after the company was established, their first locomotive was built and production continued until 1867. In 1869 the works was acquired by the Fairlie Engine & Steam Carriage Company and five further locomotives were built all to Robert Fairlie's patent. Closure took place in 1872 and it appears that about 250 locomotives were constructed.

⑯

See note 9¹/₈" x 6⁷/₈"

THE FALCON ENGINE
& CAR WORKS
Loughborough

As a result of financial difficulties in the early 1880s the firm of Henry Hughes & Company, which had been founded in 1865, was reborn in the guise of the Falcon Railway Plant Works but in 1889 this too was taken over and became The Brush Electrical Engineering Company. Initially Falcon used an oval plate with raised lettering, based on the pattern introduced by Hughes circa 1877, but replaced this with a larger oval in two versions.

Raised Brass 13" x 7"

Raised Brass 13¹/₄" x 7¹/₄"

THE FESTINIOG RAILWAY COMPANY
Boston Lodge Works, Porthmadog

A horse and gravity worked mineral railway was opened between Porthmadog and Blaenau Ffestiniog on 20th April 1836. Locomotives were introduced in 1863 and a regular passenger service commenced in 1865. Since 1836 workshops at Boston Lodge have undertaken all heavy repairs and extensive rebuilds to the Company's stock and have also occasionally undertaken completely new construction. The first new locomotive left the shops in 1879 followed by others in 1885, 1979 and 1992. All have been 0-4-4-0 tanks of Fairlie's Patent design.

Raised   Brass   14¹/₈" x 8³/₈"

FLETCHER JENNINGS & COMPANY
Lowca Works, Whitehaven

Fletcher Jennings & Company, were the successors of Tulk & Ley which had its origins in a business founded by Thomas Heslop in 1763. The firm traded under this title from 1857 to 1884, when it became Lowca Engineering Company Limited.

Raised   Brass   11" x 4¹/₄"

Raised   Not known   11¹/₄" x 6¹/₂"

FMB ENGINEERING LIMITED
Oakhanger, Bordon

The firm was formed as a partnership in March 1989 and became a Limited Company in April 1991. The first locomotive's frame was cut in 1990 and is due for completion during 1995. Three others are also under construction. All these machines will be 15" gauge full size replicas of Sir Arthur Heywood's 0-4-0T 'Katie' which originally worked on the Duke of Westminster's estate at Eaton Hall.

Raised   Plastic   3³/₈" x 2¹/₂"

JOHN FOWLER & COMPANY LIMITED
Steam Plough Works, Leeds

In 1850 John Fowler established his business to manufacture machinery mainly for the farming industry, and it was not until his death in 1866 that the first locomotives were produced. These were six 0-6-0s for the London Chatham & Dover Railway and, although other main line orders followed, the emphasis gradually moved to industrial and narrow gauge engines the last big order for standard gauge steam locomotives being executed in 1885/86. Their narrow gauge products went to many countries, including Australia, Chile, Egypt and South Africa. It appears that the last steam locomotive left the works in the mid-1930s and it is estimated that in total some 200-300 were built. Many internal combustion locomotives of various gauges were produced between 1923 and 1968, when this side of the business ceased owing to adverse trading conditions.

Up until the end of the Second World War the series of progressive numbers used for the locomotives included other products hence the very high figures shown on their plates. A separate numbering scheme was then introduced for locomotives only comprising a series of progressive numbers with seven digits. The first three figures of these denoted the class of locomotive and the other four its number within the class, so for example No.4210003 was the third member of Class 421 to be built. Shortly after the introduction of this new numbering scheme the shape of the builders' plate changed from oval to a winged rectangle.

Raised   Brass   12" x 7⁷/₈"

(17)

Raised   Brass   12" x 8"

Raised   Brass   11⁷/₈" x 7⁷/₈"

Raised   Brass   11⁷/₈" x 7⁷/₈"

Raised   Brass   11⁷/₈" x 7⁷/₈"

Raised   Brass   18⁷/₈" x 3¹/₂"

Raised   Brass   19" x 3¹/₂"

Raised   Brass/Chromed   19" x 3½"

FOX WALKER
& COMPANY

Atlas Engine Works, Bristol

Fox Walker & Company built locomotives mainly for industrial use, and between 1864 and 1879 constructed 263. Their products were built not only for the home market but also for such diverse destinations as Argentina, Holland, Java, Spain, Sudan, Sweden and Tasmania. Several tram locomotives were also built as well as a number of stationary steam engines, pumping engines and winding engines. In 1880 the firm was acquired by Thomas Peckett and became the well known concern of Peckett & Sons.

FOX, WALKER & Cº
Nº 242
ATLAS ENGINE WORKS
1874
BRISTOL

Engraved   Brass   Not known

Raised   Brass   12¾" x 9¾"

GEC TRACTION
LIMITED

Vulcan Works, Newton-le-Willows

The General Electric Company was formed in 1889. In 1968 they absorbed The English Electric Company Limited and continued to produce locomotives at Newton-le-Willows.

A number were also built under sub-contract overseas, particularly by the Union Carriage & Wagon Co. in Nigel, South Africa, and these were allocated progressive numbers within the GECT series, which themselves were a continuation of those used by English Electric.

GECT plates, which began to be used from about 1972, show their direct ancestry to the English Electric standard plates. However, worthy of mention is an oddity in the form of the 1969 example. The locomotive from which it was removed was built by English Electric but rebuilt by GECT in 1975 and fitted with a replacement GECT builders' plate carrying the English Electric progressive number.

Raised   Aluminium   14⅛" x 6⅛"

Raised   Brass   10¼" x 4½"

Raised   Brass   9" x 4"

Raised   Aluminium   10⅛" x 4½"

Raised   Brass/Chromed   10⅛" x 4½"

THOMAS GREEN & SON
LIMITED

Smithfield Ironworks, Leeds

Thomas Green's commenced building locomotives in the early 1880s and from then until 1920 produced nearly 200 tram and tank locomotives.

Raised   Brass   13¾" x 8¼"

GRANT, RITCHIE
& COMPANY LIMITED

Townholme Engine Works, Kilmarnock

Forty-five locomotives were produced between 1879 and 1920 by this firm, whose main output was colliery equipment.

Raised   Brass   10" x 6"

Raised   Brass   9⅞" x 6½"

Raised   Cast Iron   19" x 9"

GREENWOOD & BATLEY LIMITED

Albion Works, Leeds

The firm was established in 1856 as general engineers, and in 1878 built a tram locomotive, which does not appear to have been a success. They entered seriously into the building business in 1927 and produced numerous electric and battery locomotives, including flameproof designs for use in mines. Their name was shortened to Greenbat Limited in 1973, although the word Greenbat had appeared on their builders' plates for some years prior to this change. In 1980 Hunslet Holdings Limited acquired the company.

Raised   Brass   9⅝" x 5⅜"

Raised   Brass   10⅜" x 4⅝"

Raised   Brass   14" x 6"

R. & W. HAWTHORN LESLIE & CO LTD

Forth Banks Works
Newcastle-upon-Tyne

The origins of this firm date back to the earliest days of railways, when Robert Hawthorn established his business in 1817 at Forth Banks Works, Newcastle. At first they built marine engines, but in 1831 commenced the production of locomotives. In 1885 they amalgamated with A. Leslie & Company of Hebburn, who were shipbuilders, and in 1937 with Robert Stephenson & Company Limited of Darlington.

Raised   Brass   12¼" x 7"

Engraved   Brass   10½" x 3¼"

Raised   Brass   Not known

Raised   Brass   13" x 7½"

Raised   Brass   12⅞" x 7⅜"

Raised   Brass   12⅛" x 7⅞"

Raised   Brass   11¼" x 7½"

Raised   Brass   5⅞" x 3⅞"

Raised   Brass   13⅛" x 8½"

Raised   Brass   13" x 8½"

Raised   Brass   13" x 9¾"

R.&W.HAWTHORN.LESLIE&C⁰L"
3685 ENGINEERS 1925
NEWCASTLE on TYNE

| Raised | Brass | Not known |

R&W.HAWTHORN
3700
NEWCASTLE ON TYNE
1928
LESLIE & C⁰ L™

| Raised | Brass | 10¹/₈" x 6¹/₈" |

R&W.HAWTHORN
ENGINEERS
3767
ENGLAND
1930
NEWCASTLE-ON-TYNE
LESLIE & C⁰. L™.

| Raised | Brass | 6" x 4" |

R&W.HAWTHORN
3816
NEWCASTLE on TYNE
1934
LESLIE & C⁰ L™.

| Raised | Brass | 6" x 4" |

R&W.HAWTHORN.
ENGINEERS.
3873 - 1936
NEWCASTLE on TYNE
LESLIE & C⁰. LTD.

| Raised | Brass | 13" x 8¹/₂" |

R&W.HAWTHORN
ENGINEERS
2812 REBUILT 1957
NEWCASTLE on TYNE
LESLIE & C⁰.L™.

| Raised | Brass | 11⁷/₈" x 7⁵/₈" |

HEAD, WRIGHTSON & CO
Teesdale Ironworks, Stockton-on-Tees

Head, Wrightson & Company were producers of all kinds of ironwork for blast furnaces, rolling mills and collieries and builders of bridges, roofs and hydraulic machinery. In the 1860s and 1870s they turned their hand to constructing locomotives and, although some of their adverts depicted an 0-4-0ST, it seems their output was restricted to a few vertical boilered machines of two different types.

HEAD WRIGHTSON & Co
No 21
TEESDALE IRON WORKS
STOCKTON on TEES
1870

| Raised | Cast Iron | 10¹/₂" x 7¹/₂" |

SIR ARTHUR P. HEYWOOD
Duffield Bank Works, Duffield

Six 15" gauge locomotives were built at Duffield Bank between 1875 and 1916. All were tank locomotives two being 0-4-0, three 0-6-0 and one 0-8-0.

DUFFIELD BANK
1916
WORKS

| Raised | Brass | 6¹/₄" x 4¹/₄" |

HAWTHORNS & COMPANY
Leith Engine Works, Leith

In view of difficulties of shipping locomotives to Scotland by sea, R. & W. Hawthorn of Newcastle-upon-Tyne set up a business in Leith. Once the rail link from England to Scotland was completed in 1850 the factory was sold, but locomotives continued to be built by the new owners Hawthorns & Company for about a further thirty years.

A curious and, as far as is known, unique practice by this firm is worthy of mention. In some cases their builders' plates carried the date of construction in Roman numerals, and one can imagine the head scratching that must have gone on amongst those of the railway fraternity who lacked a knowledge of these.

HAWTHORNS & Cº
No 240
S.D.DAVISONS PATENT
1861
LEITH

| Engraved | Brass | 11¹/₈" x 8¹/₈" |

MDCCCLXXXIII
S.D.DAVISON'S
HAWTHORNS & Cº
PATENT
LEITH

| Engraved | Brass | 12" x 9" |

No138
HAWTHORNS & Cº LEITH ENGINE WORKS
1856.

| Raised | Brass | 31³/₈" x 6¹/₄" |

ROBERT HEATH & SONS LIMITED

Biddulph, Stoke-on-Trent

Robert Heath & Sons Limited is believed to have built about ten locomotives for their own use between 1888 and 1926. Shortly after the First World War the company's title changed to Robert Heath & Low Moor Limited.

Raised	Brass	14⁵/₈" x 8"

Raised	Brass	14¹/₂" x 8"

Raised	Cast Iron	16³/₄" x 9³/₄"

F. C. HIBBERD & COMPANY LIMITED

Park Royal Works, London

After taking over the design and patents of J. & F. Howard Ltd, of Bedford in 1931, Hibberd's moved into their Park Royal Works in 1932 and began building locomotives under the 'Planet' trademark which appeared on their builders' plates. 'Planet' locomotives were first produced after the First World War by the Kent Construction & Engineering Co Ltd, of Ashford in Kent, and had been built at two other works before Hibberd commenced construction in 1932. By 1964 the manufacturing rights had been acquired by the Butterley Engineering Co Ltd, of Ripley after the take-over of F. C. Hibberd Limited, by the Butterley Group.

Raised	Brass	4³/₄" x 1¹/₄"

Raised	Brass	6" x 3³/₄"

Raised	Brass/Chromed	12" x 7¹/₂"

THOMAS HILL (ROTHERHAM) LIMITED

Vanguard Works, Kilnhurst

Although the firm was founded in 1937, it was not until 1960 that Thomas Hill built their first diesel locomotive, utilising the frames of a Sentinel steam locomotive. Many of their early products were similar conversions and these were identified by the letter 'C' (for conversion) after the progressive number. Later locomotives which were built as new were identified by the letter 'V' for Vanguard, the registered name under which they were manufactured. The firm became a Rolls-Royce subsidiary in 1963. After just thirty years in this trade, the company was sold and the business was carried on by RFS Engineering Limited. As from the beginning of 1992 some major changes in the structure of the RFS Industries Group resulted in the operation at Kilnhurst becoming a separate trading unit known as RFS Locomotives. This lasted until the middle of May 1993 when the works closed.

Three patterns of builders' plate are known, the last variety with a leopard logo being introduced about 1985.

Raised	Brass	7¹/₂" x 4¹/₂"

Raised	Brass	7¹/₂" x 4¹/₂"

Raised	Brass	8" x 3¹/₂"

(8)

Raised	Brass	5³/₄" x 3⁵/₈"

JAMES & FREDK. HOWARD LIMITED

Britannia Iron Works, Bedford

Prior to becoming bankrupt in 1931, Howard's produced a number of internal combustion locomotives. In 1932 the works was taken over by Britannia Iron & Steel Works Limited.

Raised	Brass	9⁵/₈" x 6¹/₂"

HUDSWELL, CLARKE & COMPANY LIMITED
Railway Foundry, Leeds

In 1860 Messrs W. S. Hudswell and J. Clarke founded the company of Hudswell & Clarke as general engineers but from 1861 their principal business became the production of locomotives. Between 1870 and 1881 the firm traded under the title of Hudswell, Clarke & Rodgers but upon the departure of the latter gentleman became Hudswell, Clarke & Company. During 1899 the firm acquired limited liability status. In the late 1960s the Trind Group of companies obtained Hudswell's and between 1970 and 1972 continued to produce locomotives as Hudswell Badger Limited. They soon sold their locomotive interests, however, to The Hunslet Engine Company Limited who from 1976 to 1982 constructed locomotives to Hudswell's designs on their own premises across the road from the Hudswell workshops. The machines built under this arrangement were given Hunslet works numbers but did not carry plates bearing that firm's name. Instead, and rather curiously, they were fitted with standard Hudswell, Clarke & Company Limited plates which continued that company's series of progressive numbers. The last few plates fitted to these Hunslet/Hudswell locomotives had the words 'Railway Foundry' deleted from them as if in recognition that a long tradition had at last ended.

Hudswell's initial builder's plates were rectangular, but in the early 1880s they introduced their first version of the familiar brass oval with recessed lettering, which continued in use for nearly eighty years. There were, of course, exceptions to the rule particularly numerous examples being the small brass oval plates with raised lettering used mainly on diesel mining locomotives after the Second World War and the later large brass oval with raised lettering that replaced the brass oval with recessed lettering in the early 1960s.

Hudswell's used a separate series of progressive numbers for steam and diesel production, the latter being prefixed by D (or in at least one case by DE) for surface machines and DM for mines locomotives. In all they produced over 1800 steam locomotives and about 900 non-steam. Of the non-steam, 11 were built with Hudswell Badger plates and 27 by Hunslet with Hudswell plates.

Engraved   Brass   14½" x 5¾"

Engraved   Brass   14⅜" x 5¾"

Engraved   Brass   14¼" x 5⅝"

Engraved   Brass   12½" x 7¾"

Raised/Engraved Brass   13¼" x 8¼"

Raised/Engraved Brass   13⅛" x 8⅜"

Engraved   Brass   10¾" x 6¼"

Engraved   Brass   12⅞" x 8⅛"

Engraved   Brass   12⅞" x 8"

Engraved   Brass   12¾" x 8"

Raised   Brass   13⅜" x 7¾"

Engraved   Brass   6⅛" x 4⅝"

| Engraved | Brass | 10¼" x 5¾" |

63

| Engraved | Brass | 12⅞" x 8⅛" |

| Raised | Cast Iron | 11⅜" x 8⅛" |

| Engraved | Brass | 12⅞" x 8⅛" |

| Engraved | Brass | 11⅜" x 5¼" |

| Engraved | Brass | 10¼" x 5¾" |

| Engraved | Brass | 10⅜" x 5⅞" |

| Raised | Brass | 13" x 8⅛" |

| Engraved | Brass | 12⅞" x 8⅛" |

| Engraved | Brass | 8⅛" x 4" |

| Raised | Brass | 8⅛" x 4⅛" |

| Engraved | Brass | 12¾" x 8" |

| Engraved | Brass | 13" x 8⅛" |

| Engraved | Brass | 10⅜" x 5⅞" |

36

HUDSWELL CLARKE & Cº Lᵀᴰ
1815
RAILWAY FOUNDRY
1948
LEEDS. ENGLAND.

| Raised | Brass | 8¼" x 4⅛" |

| Raised | Brass | 8¼" x 4⅛" |

Engraved — Brass — 12⅝" x 8"

Raised — Brass — 12¾" x 8⅛"

Raised — Brass — 8⅛" x 4⅛"

Raised — Brass — 8¼" x 4⅛"

 ③⑥

HUDSWELL CLARKE & Cº LTD
DM1450
1982
LEEDS. ENGLAND.

Raised — Brass — 8¼" x 4⅛"

ROBERT HUDSON LIMITED
Gildersome Foundry, Morley, Leeds

Hudson's was founded in 1865 and became well known as suppliers of light railway equipment particularly to overseas countries. A few internal combustion machines appear to have been constructed but normally locomotive building work was undertaken by outside contractors such as Kerr Stuart & Company Limited, The Hunslet Engine Company Limited and Hudswell, Clarke & Company Limited, on behalf of the company.

⑳

Engraved — Brass — 7" x 5⅛"

⑳

Raised — Brass — 6" x 5"

Raised — Brass — 10½" x 5¾"

Raised — Brass — 10½" x 5¾"

HENRY HUGHES & COMPANY
Falcon Works, Loughborough

The firm of Henry Hughes & Company was founded in 1865, and it appears that the first locomotive was produced very shortly thereafter. A substantial part of their business appears to have been the supply of tram locomotives and 0-4-0STs mainly for contractors. In 1883 the company became the Falcon Railway Plant Works.

Engraved — Brass — 9" x 5¾"

THE HUNSLET ENGINE COMPANY LIMITED
Leeds

The Hunslet Engine Company was formed in 1864 by M J. T. Leather, and a factory was built on the site wher once had stood the workshops of the ill-fated firm of E. B Wilson. It was quite a bold decision, considering tha there were already three other builders established in th area (Hudswell Clarke, Kitson and Manning Wardle) b obviously Mr Leather thought there was room for anoth er. Indeed so well did this firm adapt itself to its trade an to market trends that it still survives to this day. In 1902 became a limited company with the title The Hunsle Engine Company Limited, and during 1909 completed i 1000th locomotive, a 2-4-2T for the Baraset-Basirh Light Railway in India. Many tank locomotives were bui over the years, of different designs and gauges, inte spersed with orders for tender engines, but without dou the most unusual machines to leave the workshops wer the three that were completed in 1887 for the Listowel Ballybunion Railway, which was a monorail.

In the dark years of the depression in the early 193C Hunslet's ventured into the field of diesel power, a mov which was to stand them in good stead to the presen day. The last steam locomotive was built in 1971 to th design of Kerr Stuart's 0-4-2T 'Brazil' for a narrow gaug forestry line in Indonesia, thus bringing to an end a lon association of more than a century with that type of trac tion. Its builders' plate reads 'The Hunslet Engin Company Limited, Leeds, For Robert Hudson Limite Leeds, 9" x 15", No.3902, 1971'. (See illustration).

Diesel production was at first included in the sam series of progressive numbers as the steam locomotive but after the Second World War, with the obvious declin ing market for steam, the diesels were numbere separately in a series of their own commencing at 400C

For a while, in recent years, the company traded und the title Hunslet Holdings Plc but has since reverted The Hunslet Engine Company Limited.

Engraved | Brass | Not known

Engraved | Brass | 9½" x 6⅝"

Engraved | Brass | 15⅛" x 9½"

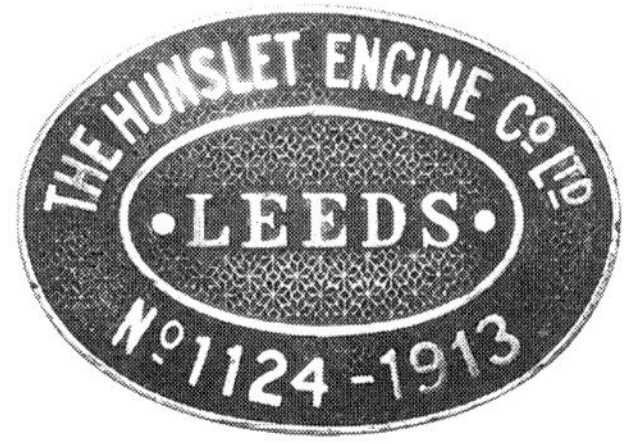

Raised | Brass | 10⅞" x 7⅝"

Raised | Cast Iron | 11¼" x 8⅛"

(22)

Raised | Brass | 11⅛" x 7⅞"

Raised | Brass | 11½" x 8"

Raised | Brass | 11½" x 8⅛"

Raised | Brass | 11½" x 8"

Raised | Brass | 11½" x 8⅛"

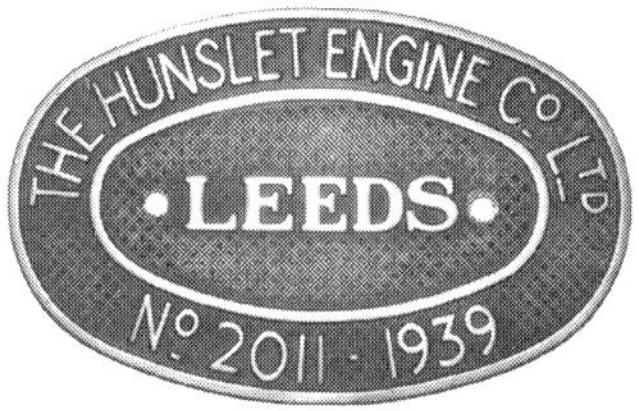

Raised | Brass | 8" x 5"

(37)

THE HUNSLET ENGINE CO. LTD.
FOR
ROBERT HUDSON LTD,
LEEDS.
2645 1941

Raised | Brass | 4½" x 2½"

Raised | Cast Iron | 14⅛" x 8"

Raised | Brass | 4½" x 2½"

Raised | Brass | 11¼" x 8"

(23)

Raised | Cast Iron | 11¼" x 8"

(24)

Raised   Brass   11½" x 8"

Engraved   Brass   6" x 4½"

Raised   Brass   11½" x 8"

Engraved   Brass   5⅞" x 3½"

Raised   Brass   11⅛" x 7⅞"

Raised   Aluminium   15⅜" x 9¾"

Raised   Brass   11½" x 8"

Raised   Brass   11½" x 8"

(58)

Raised   Brass   11½" x 8"

Engraved   Brass   6" x 2⅜"

Raised   Brass   11⅜" x 8"

Raised   Brass   11⅜" x 8"

(25)

Raised   Brass   10" x 6½"

(59)

Raised   Brass   11½" x 8"

Engraved   Brass   6" x 3½"

(60)

Engraved   Brass   5⅞" x 3½"

| Raised | Brass | 6" x 4" |

| Raised | Brass | 11½" x 8⅛" |

| Raised | Brass | 11¾" x 8⅛" |

| REPAIRED & MODIFIED
BY THE
HUNSLET ENGINE CO. LTD.
LEEDS
N° 5917 — NOV 1963 | | |

| Engraved | Brass | 5" x 3" |

| Raised | Brass | 10½" x 4" |

| Raised | Brass | Not known |

| Engraved | Brass | 6" x 3½" |

| Engraved | Brass | 6" x 3" |

| Engraved | Brass | 5⅞" x 6¼" |

ALAN KEEF LIMITED
Lea Line, Ross on Wye

Alan Keef began his light railway business at Cote Farm, near Bampton in Oxfordshire, in the early 1970s, but in November 1986 the firm moved to its present premises at Lea Line. The firm became a limited company on 1st December 1975, and produced its first locomotive the following year. By mid 1992 over forty locomotives had been built, including a narrow gauge steam engine for a pleasure line in Holland. The 'Diamond K' logo was introduced in 1976, but has been used in its cast builders' plate form only since locomotive No.23 was built in 1988.

| Raised | Brass | 9⅝" x 6⅜" |

KERR, STUART
& COMPANY LIMITED
California Works, Stoke-on-Trent

Kerr Stuart had its origins in the firm of James Kerr & Company, which was founded in Glasgow in 1881, and carried on the trade of rolling stock and permanent way contractors. Their catalogue offered everything from signals to locomotives, but its seems likely that they acted simply as agents for other people's products. It was therefore somewhat of an enterprising step when in 1892 they went into the business of locomotive manufacturing for themselves by purchasing the general engineering works of Hartley, Arnoux & Fanning at Stoke-on-Trent, and severed their links with Glasgow. At this time the locomotive trade was extremely competitive so it was not without some risk that this decision was taken. The firm soon acquired a high reputation as a builder of both main line and industrial types, and during their comparatively short existence turned out about 1500 in all (alterations in the sequence of progressive numbers make it difficult to calculate the exact number with any accuracy). Sad to say that in 1930 California Works was forced to close, not because of any direct effect of the recession but because their Chairman, unknown to the other directors, had used the firm's good name and credit to back a highly speculative venture which had failed, resulting in the compulsory winding up of the company.

Several sizes and styles of oval plate were used, some without building dates and others with 'Ltd' abbreviated to 'Ld'. Many carried reference to their London office.

| Raised | Brass | 6" x 4" |

Raised   Brass   9⅞" x 6¼"

Raised   Brass   12¾" x 6¾"

KITSON & COMPANY LIMITED

Airedale Foundry, Leeds

James Kitson's Airedale Foundry was established in 1835 and was thus one of the earliest locomotive workshops. In the beginning only parts were manufactured for other builders, but in 1838 the first locomotive was produced. Its removal from the workshops borders on farce, as a wall of the building had to be removed in order to extract it. The name of the firm was changed frequently during the early years – James Kitson, Todd, Kitson & Laird, Kitson & Laird, Laird & Kitson, Kitson Thompson & Hewitson, Kitson & Hewitson and finally, circa 1864, Kitson & Company. The firm, up to the time it ceased to build locomotives in 1938, constructed over 5000, both for railways at home and abroad. Unlike the other builders in Leeds, however, many of these were for main line work rather than industrial use. Interesting types produced include Kitson-Meyer articulated locomotives, of which over fifty were built mainly between 1903 and 1913 (the last two, which were 2-8-8-2s, were despatched to the Girardot Railway in 1935) and the 1924 built experimental Kitson–Still 2-6-2T which was a hybrid steam/diesel machine. Despite much perseverance, the experiment was a failure and the financial commitment to the project at a time of dwindling orders did little to help the Company. In 1934 the receiver was called in, but despite efforts to revive the firm, locomotive building finished in 1938 and the Company ceased trading in 1945.

Raised   Brass   11⅞" x 6⅞"

Raised   Brass   13¼" x 5¾"

THE KILMARNOCK ENGINEERING CO LTD

Britannia Works, Kilmarnock

The Kilmarnock Engineering Company Limited were successors to Dick Kerr & Company and built seven locomotives in or around 1920. Their progressive numbers commenced at No.500 and finished at No.526, the gaps presumably being filled by other types of machinery.

Engraved   Brass   10¾" x 6⅜"

Raised   Brass   12¾" x 6¾"

Raised   Brass   21⅝" x 7½"

Engraved   Brass   6⅛" x 3½"

(26)

Raised   Brass   6" x 4"

Raised   Brass   14½" x 7¾"

Engraved   Brass   35½" x 6"

Engraved   Brass   17¾" x 3"

Raised   Cast Iron   10½" x 6¼"

Raised   Cast Iron   6¹⁄₈" x 4"

Engraved   Brass   10⁵⁄₈" x 6³⁄₈"

Raised   Brass   10³⁄₄" x 6¹⁄₈"

Raised   Brass   12³⁄₄" x 8"

KNIGHTLEY LIGHT RAILWAY
Knightley, Stafford

Roger Greatrex, the proprietor of the Knightley Light Railway, commenced operations in 1980 and built his first locomotive in 1982. Between then and 1992 ten locomotives had been constructed all of 7¹⁄₄" gauge. These comprised two steam locomotives, a 'Royal Scot' and a Bagnall 0-6-0 tank based on Kerr, Stuart's 'Haig' class, and eight petrol hydrostatics of such diverse designs as Bagnall 0-6-0 diesels, General Motors' GP40's and a Thomas the Tank Engine look-alike. Construction has also included wagons, coaches and miscellaneous railway items such as turntables, points, point levers and railbenders.

Initially, builders' plates were rectangular brass with engraved lettering, but later oval brass plates with raised lettering were introduced. These plates have been fitted to locomotives and rolling stock alike and progressive numbers, which started at 1001, are allocated from a common series for all such construction. Later the progressive numbers were prefixed by L, C or W to indicate locomotives, coaches or wagons.

> KNIGHTLEY LIGHT
> RAILWAY
> Nº 1001
> BUILT 1986
> LOCOMOTIVE ENGINEERS

Engraved   Brass   4" x 2"

⑧

Raised   Brass   3⁵⁄₈" x 2⁵⁄₈"

LAKE & ELLIOT LIMITED
Braintree

Lake & Elliot Limited had a foundry in Braintree and produced a small number of internal combustion locomotives. The plate illustrated is from a narrow gauge petrol mechanical locomotive built about 1924.

Raised   Cast Iron   8" x 5"

LINGFORD GARDINER & COMPANY
Railway Street, Bishop Auckland

This firm traded from the 1850s to 1931 as general engineers, but also repaired and built locomotives. Building commenced about 1900 and it appears that by the time of closure seven locomotives had been constructed.

> LINGFORD, GARDINER & Cº
> *ENGINEERS*
> BISHOP AUCKLAND.

Engraved   Brass   14" x 7"

R. A. LISTER & COMPANY LIMITED
Dursley

Lister's commenced building internal combustion locomotives in 1928, and continued in this field until 1968. The firm's title changed to Lister Blackstone Rail Traction Limited in 1957.

Raised   Brass   6³⁄₈" x 2⁵⁄₈"

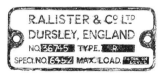

Raised   Brass   6³⁄₈" x 2⁵⁄₈"

Raised   Brass   5¹⁄₂" x 2⁷⁄₈"

THE LOGAN MINING MACHINERY CO LTD

Gray Street Works, Lochee, Dundee

From its formation in 1946 until closure in 1978 this firm produced about 270 locomotives for use in underground mines. Approximately 100 battery locomotives were built to their own specifications up to 1952, but from the following year a sub-contract arrangement was entered into with Greenwood & Batley Limited of Leeds, to build locomotives of that firm's design.

Raised   Brass   8¹⁄₈" x 5"

LOWCA ENGINEERING COMPANY LIMITED

Lowca Works, Whitehaven

In 1840, under the name of Tulk & Ley, two locomotives were constructed at Lowca Works for the Maryport & Carlisle Railway and until its takeover by Fletcher Jennings Limited in 1857 this firm built a total of 20. Fletcher Jennings continued this business and built 171 over the next 27 years, when the business became a limited company and changed its title to Lowca Engineering Company Limited. The name was again changed in 1905 to the New Lowca Engineering Company Limited, but by this time locomotive building had almost ceased and the end finally came following a serious fire at the works in 1912. In all, nearly 250 locomotives were erected at Lowca Works.

Raised   Brass   15¹⁄₂" x 11⁷⁄₈"

LOWCA ENGINEERING C° L°
N° 245
CLASS D
1906
– WHITEHAVEN –

Raised   Brass   15¹⁄₂" x 11⁷⁄₈"

NEW LOWCA ENGINEERING C° L° TD N° 250 1912

Raised   Brass   61⁷⁄₈" x 5"

MANNING WARDLE & COMPANY LIMITED

Boyne Engine Works, Leeds

It could be said that Manning Wardle rose from the ashes following the demise of the Railway Foundry of E. B. Wilson & Company and indeed some leading employees from that firm were active in establishing the new Company notably Alexander Campbell, who had been the manager prior to the Railway Foundry's closure. When the Railway Foundry estate was put up for sale, several locomotive drawings were purchased and a number of engines built to their designs down to the characteristic fluted dome and safety valve covers. Manning Wardle even went so far as to imitate the Railway Foundry's builders' plate for the first few years of their existence up to about 1871. The first locomotive was turned out in February 1859, and throughout, the company concentrated mainly on building various types of saddletanks for industrial use. Its products were generally considered to be excellent, but a failure to modernise and the recession led to the firm going into voluntary liquidation in 1927.

From the early 1870's an oval plate was adopted. At first this was engraved, but just after the turn of the century a version with raised lettering was introduced. This was interesting as it had a decorative background of the same pattern as the plates that Hunslet's began to use about this time. This would seem to indicate that the two firms were using the same source for the supply of these. The background design, which is generally referred to as the 'Yorkshire Rose' pattern, also appeared during the Second World War on the cast iron plates fitted by Hudswell Clarke to their Austerity 0-6-0ST's.

The Manning Wardle plates listed are shown in progressive number sequence and not by date.

Engraved   Brass   10³⁄₄" x 6"

Raised   Brass   13" x 8¹⁄₈"

Engraved   Brass   10⁷⁄₈" x 6"

MANNING.WARDLE & C° N° 241 LEEDS. 1867

Engraved   Brass   23⁵⁄₈" x 5⁷⁄₈"

Raised   Brass   10³⁄₄" x 6¹⁄₄"

| Engraved | Brass | 10⁵/₈" x 5⁷/₈" |

| Raised | Brass | 6" x 3³/₄" |

| Raised | Aluminium | 15¹/₄" x 9³/₄" |

| Raised | Brass | 13⁵/₈" x 8⁷/₈" |

MARKHAM & CO LTD
Broad Oaks Iron Works, Chesterfield

In 1889, just before being bought by Markham's, Oliver & Company Limited completed two 0-4-0STs and both of these appear to have carried builders' plates with that firm's title. Markham & Company Limited continued this line of business and between 1891 and 1914 built a further seventeen locomotives. Of the nineteen built at Broad Oaks Iron Works only the first eleven were allocated progressive numbers commencing at 101, but not all builders' plates carried these.

| Engraved | Brass | 11" x 6¹/₈" |

| Raised | Brass | 10³/₄" x 6" |

(39)

| Raised | Brass | 13⁵/₈" x 8⁷/₈" |

MARTYN BROTHERS
Chapelside Works, Airdrie

In the last decade of the nineteenth century this company built between two and six steam locomotives for use at collieries, and these engines were based on designs by Dick & Stevenson, whose drawings Martyn Brothers acquired on the closure of the Airdrie Engine Works in 1890.

| Raised | Brass | 10⁷/₈" x 6³/₈" |

| Raised | Brass | 10⁷/₈" x 6¹/₈" |

| Engraved | Brass | 15¹/₂" x 7⁵/₈" |

(41)

| Raised | Brass | 10⁷/₈" x 6¹/₄" |

MANNING, WARDLE & Cᵒ Lᵀᴰ
REBUILT 1939
2000
R. STEPHENSON & HAWTHORNS
LEEDS. 1921

| Raised | Brass | 10³/₄" x 6" |

MARKHAM & Cᵒ LIMᵀᴰ
Nᵒ 109.
BROAD OAKS IRON WORKS
1894.
CHESTERFIELD.

| Engraved | Brass | 15¹/₂" x 7⁵/₈" |

| Raised | Brass | 8" x 4⁷/₈" |

MAXITRAK LIMITED
Staplehurst, Maidstone

Since producing their first locomotive in June 1978 it is believed that by mid 1993 over 1000 had been supplied, mainly in the form of machined kits. These have included both steam and electric machines mostly of 5" and 7¼" gauge, with a few of 3½" and one of 15" gauge.

Electric locomotives are given progressive numbers between 100-999, and steam between 001-099 and 1000 onwards. The small oval plate depicted is fitted to 5" gauge locomotives and under, the larger oval plate to 7¼" gauge and the rhomboid shaped plate to 'sit in' locomotives of 7¼" to 15" gauge.

⑧

Raised	Brass	1" x ¾"

⑧

Raised	Brass	2⅝" x 1¾"

⑧
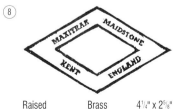

Raised	Brass	4¼" x 2⅝"

McCULLOCH SONS & KENNEDY LIMITED
Vulcan Works, Kilmarnock

In 1847 Thomas McCulloch purchased from the Duke of Portland some land, and on this site erected the Vulcan Works, to which he transferred his engineering business. The firm of Thomas McCulloch & Sons became a limited liability company under the title of McCulloch Sons & Kennedy Limited in May 1889 and shortly thereafter appear to have built at least one or possibly two locomotives. Some mystery, however, surrounds this and it could be that the No.324 carried on the builders' plate has something to do with the Barclays & Company series of progressive numbers, the highest known of which is 322.

Raised	Brass	10⅞" x 5"

McEWAN PRATT & COMPANY LIMITED
Wickford

Petrol locomotives and railcars were produced by this firm, but in 1913 the business was acquired by Baguley's of Burton-on-Trent, who continued to use the company's name for trading purposes.

Raised	Brass	7" x 4½"

MILNER ENGINEERING (CHESTER) LIMITED
Higher Kinnerton

The Company was started in 1972, and the first locomotive built commercially was a 7¼" gauge 'Hunslet'. By mid-1993 about thirty large scale locomotives had been constructed and numerous rebuilds undertaken. Gauges have ranged from 5" to 12¼" and production has included two half full size 12¼" gauge, narrow gauge prototypes, an East African Railways Class 59 Beyer-Garratt in 7¼" gauge (now in the National Railway Museum, York) and a one third full size Tasmanian Railways' Beyer-Garratt. The Company has always specialised in steam engines and has never built any diesel locomotives. In addition to building locomotives they have supplied, over the years, a complete range of equipment for miniature railways, and were involved in the sale and reconstruction of the Fairbourne Miniature Railway and, in 1993, were associated with the design and promotion of a multi-million pound miniature railway centre.

The standard plate shown is generally used and is painted either with a red or black background. In some cases, however, the Company name has been included on other plates associated with the locomotive. For example on their standard 7¼" gauge Denver & Rio Grande locomotive the Baldwin smokebox door plate had 'MILNER ENGINEERING (CHESTER) LTD KINNERTON U.K.' instead of the Baldwin company name.

Raised	Brass	4" x 2¾"

METROPOLITAN-VICKERS ELECTRICAL COMPANY LIMITED
Manchester and Stockton-on-Tees

The company was formed in 1919 by a group of British businesses headed by Vickers, who had bought the American interests in the British Westinghouse Electrical Manufacturing Company. This latter concern had recently completed the electrification of the Metropolitan Railway in London and in recognition of this the new company became Metropolitan-Vickers Limited. In 1928 the firm combined with The British Thomson-Houston Company Limited to form Associated Electrical Industries Limited, but still traded under its own name until 1958.

It should be noted that in 1949, in association with Beyer Peacock, a subsidiary company was formed titled Metropolitan-Vickers-Beyer Peacock Limited. This operated from Bowesfield Works in Stockton-on-Tees and 242 electric locomotives were produced up until 1960. This company went into voluntary liquidation early the following year due to a decline in orders.

Raised	Brass	12" x 6"

Engraved	Aluminium	5" x 1⅝"

Raised   Brass   13" x 6¾"

Raised   Brass   13" x 6¾"

Raised   Aluminium   18" x 5⅛"

Raised   Brass   13¾" x 3"

MOTOR RAIL LIMITED
Simplex Works, Bedford

The Motor Rail & Tramcar Company Limited set up business in Lewes in 1911, but in 1914 moved to Bedford. The title of the firm was changed to Motor Rail Limited in 1931. Their main output was narrow gauge diesels, although a few standard gauge machines were also built. They used the trade name 'Simplex', and this was the name generally used when referring to their locomotives. The works closed in the late 1980s when they were trading as Simplex Mechanical Handling Limited.

Raised   Cast Iron   11¼" x 7¾"

Raised   Brass   7⅞" x 3"

Raised   Brass   7⅝" x 2⅞"

Raised   Brass   7⅝" x 2⅝"

(8)

Printed   Aluminium   7⅝" x 2¾"

(8)

Printed   Aluminium   7⅝" x 2¾"

MUIR HILL ENGINEERING LIMITED
Trafford Park, Manchester

For several years from around the early 1920s Muir Hill produced locomotives based on Fordson tractors. Some were little more than conversion jobs which were often not heavy enough to carry out their duties. By the end of that decade an improved design had been evolved, using a Fordson power plant mounted on a more substantial chassis and an improved gearbox giving two speed drive in both forward and reverse directions.

Raised   Cast Iron   8½" x 5½"

NASMYTH WILSON & COMPANY LIMITED
Bridgewater Foundry, Manchester

In 1836 James Nasmyth established the Bridgewater Foundry and in 1839 produced his first steam locomotive. For many years a side-line, not until the 1880s did locomotive manufacturing begin to expand. Many were for export, only 119 out of 1307 constructed between 1873 and 1938 being for the home market. The depression in the 1930s took its toll and by 1939 the Company, having produced 1531 locomotives, had gone to the wall. The firm had several changes of title: Nasmyth Gaskell & Company, James Nasmyth & Company, Patricroft Iron Works, Nasmyth Wilson & Company, and finally in 1882 Nasmyth Wilson & Company Limited. When the Company ceased to use the workshops, the Ministry of Supply took over and it became Patricroft Royal Ordnance Factory.

Nasmyth's originally used an oval plate, but in 1905 turned to a very distinctive triangular pattern plate.

| Raised | Brass | 11³/₄" x 7¹/₂" |

| Raised | Brass | 13⁷/₈" x 5¹/₂" |

(27)

NATIONAL COAL BOARD
Philadelphia Workshops, Co. Durham

The works at Philadelphia were originally set up to undertake general repair work for the Earl of Durham's Lambton Collieries and to carry out overhauls of their locomotives. A few locomotives were, however, built between 1877 and 1894, but no further new construction took place after that date. The works finally closed under British Coal ownership on Friday 22nd December 1989.

The number shown on the plate below is basically an accountancy device which shows that the locomotive concerned was repaired during the 1980/81 financial year, that it was a surface locomotive (plant identification code 601) and that it was the second machine to be dealt with during that period.

| Raised | Brass | 15¹/₈" x 7⁷/₈" |

NORTH BRITISH
LOCOMOTIVE CO LTD
Atlas, Hyde Park
and Queen's Park Works, Glasgow

At the turn of the century there was keen competition amongst locomotive builders, so much so that traditional overseas markets for British locomotives were being threatened, particularly by American firms. Much scorn was poured on the American products to try to belittle them, but American efficiency and an ability not only to produce the article more cheaply but also on time led to the Glasgow builders Neilson Reid, Dübs and Sharp Stewart writing a joint letter to The Times in defence of their honour. Their action had little effect and their old customers still continued to desert them, preferring to buy where they could obtain locomotives both quickly and at less cost. Something more positive had to be done to combat this menace and thus it was that in February 1903 the three former rivals amalgamated to form the largest locomotive building company outside America. At first it was intended that the new combine should be called The British Locomotive Company, but as they found that there was another engineering firm trading under that name they became the North British Locomotive Company. The progressive numbers of the three firms were added together to form the first number of the new Company and the combine began to flourish, so much so that by 1914 they had built their 5000th locomotive. The variety they produced was tremendous and ranged from 'King Arthurs', 'Royal Scots', 'Sandringhams' and 'Jubilees' for the home market to Mallet Compounds, 4-8-4 condensing locomotives and 4-8-2 + 2-8-4 Garratts (under sub-contract from Beyer-Peacock) for overseas. Atlas Works ceased production in 1923 owing to there being insufficient orders to keep the erecting shops fed and all construction was then concentrated at the other two works. After the Second World War the future looked good, but the decline in steam on the world's railways and the failure of the Company to come to terms successfully with the diesel and electric age led to its going into voluntary liquidation in 1962. Like Beyer-Peacock, NBL had backed hydraulic transmission and that, together with intense competition from America, spelt the end.

The result of the amalgamation produced new plates based on the old style patterns used by the three constituent firms. The Dübs diamond turned into NBL, Glasgow Locomotive Works and then Queen's Park Works and finally for the last twenty years of the Company's existence into their exclusive trademark on which no works of origin was shown. Neilson Reid's oval evolved into the familiar round NBL Hyde Park Works and Sharp Stewart's oval continued much as before, save for showing the new NBL title. Not surprisingly within this framework, with such a large output, other variations were from time to time to be found.

| Raised | Brass | 13³/₈" x 5³/₈" |

| Raised | Brass | 10¹/₈" x 5³/₈" |

| Raised | Brass | 9¹/₂" x 6¹/₈" |

| Raised | Brass | 12⁷/₈" x 5¹/₄" |

| Raised | Brass | 7³/₄" diameter |

| Raised | Brass | 15¹/₈" x 6¹/₄" |

| Engraved | Brass | 11¹/₂" x 4³/₄" |

Raised   Brass $7^5/_8$" diameter

Engraved   Brass $6^1/_4$" diameter

(28)

Raised   Brass $12^3/_4$" x $5^1/_4$"

(28)

Raised   Brass $13^3/_8$" x $5^1/_2$"

(28)

Raised   Brass $13^3/_8$" x $5^1/_2$"

Raised   Brass $13^3/_4$" x $5^5/_8$"

Raised   Brass $13^3/_4$" x $5^1/_2$"

Raised   Brass $13^5/_8$" x $5^1/_2$"

Raised   Aluminium $14^1/_8$" x $6^1/_8$"

Raised   Aluminium $13^3/_8$" x $5^1/_2$"

Raised   Aluminium $13^3/_8$" x $5^1/_2$"

NEILSON & COMPANY

Hyde Park Works, Glasgow

The origins of Neilson & Company date to around 1837, when Walter Neilson and James Mitchell went into partnership. At first they built stationary and marine engines and it was not until 1843 that they produced a locomotive. The firm had several different titles in the period until 1855 (Neilson & Mitchell; Kerr, Mitchell & Neilson; Kerr Neilson & Company; Neilson & Mitchell) when it was then known as Neilson & Company. The demand for their locomotives was so great that in 1861 work started on the building of new premises in the Springburn area, and these were called 'Hyde Park Works' after Neilson's previous establishment. A great variety of locomotive types was produced over the years but perhaps none so strange as the ice locomotive of 1861, which was designed for hauling trains of sledges across the frozen wastes of Russia. After a quarrel with James Reid, his partner Walter Neilson left the Company in 1876, and in 1884 set up the ill-fated Clyde Locomotive Works, which was soon to be acquired by Sharp Stewart. James Reid then took the helm but it was not until 1898 that the firm's name was changed to Neilson Reid & Company. Five years later it became part of the North British Locomotive Company having produced nearly 6000 locomotives.

Raised   Brass $14^1/_2$" x $8^3/_4$"

Engraved   Brass   6½" x 3⅞"

Raised   Brass   10¼" x 6"

Raised   Cast Iron   5⅞" x 3⅞"

Engraved   Brass   6" x 4"

Engraved   Brass   9" x 5½"

Raised   Brass   9⅝" x 5⅞"

Raised   Brass   9¼" x 5¾"

Raised   Brass   9" x 6⅜"

Raised   Brass   6⅝" x 4¼"

Engraved   Brass   8⅞" x 6⅜"

THE PEARSON & KNOWLES COAL & IRON COMPANY LIMITED
Dallam Forge, Warrington

It appears that twelve locomotives were built by this firm, although there is a possibility that there may have been a few others. They carried no builder's numbers on their plates.

Raised   Brass   18⅜" x 13⅝"

ALEXANDER PENNEY & COMPANY
London

Alexander Penney acted as agents for Brush and Falcon and, as will be seen their plate, although carrying their own series of numbers, is obviously based on a Falcon pattern. The plate illustrated was from a metre gauge 4-6-0 locomotive supplied to the British North Borneo State Railway.

Raised   Brass   13¼" x 7¼"

PFEIFFERBAHN MINIATURE RAILWAYS
Withnell Station, Chorley

Mr Don Fifer built his first loco in 1979 and by the middle of 1993 had constructed 18 complete machines, all of which were either petrol hydraulics or battery electrics ranging from 5" to 10¼" gauge. Progressive numbers have been allocated in a straight run from one in order of production/supply. In addition many chassis have been produced for customers to fit their own bodywork.

Engraved   Brass   2" x 1¼"

PECKETT & SONS
Atlas Works, Bristol

The business of Fox Walker & Company was taken over in 1880 by Thomas Peckett under the title of Peckett & Sons, who continued their predecessor's policy of meeting the needs of industrial railways. Their early products were quite handsome machines which sported copper capped chimneys and brass domes and safety valve covers. Much of the works output was four and six-coupled saddletanks of various designs and gauges, interspersed with a few sidetanks. The firm also supplied kits of parts to some of their customers for self assembly of the locomotives on their own premises. Around 1913 they became a limited company and this change was incorporated into the builders' plates. Altogether about 1200 steam locomotives were built.

Pecketts doggedly stuck to a steam only policy after many of their competitors had turned their attention to diesel locomotives. The excellence of their products did nothing to change the hard reality of the declining demand for steam and in 1954 they announced that they too would enter the diesel market. As a result of this, five standard gauge diesels were built, the first emerging from the workshops in 1956. They were not particularly successful having arrived too late on the scene to pose any threat to manufacturers who were already established with well tried products. In 1958 Reed Crane & Hoist Company Limited acquired the business and continued to supply spares for a while, but they too eventually ceased trading and the works closed in 1962.

On their steam locomotives the firm used oval engraved plates, which were mostly of brass with wax filled lettering, although a few cast iron examples also appeared between 1943-45. For the diesels, however, a new rectangular design with raised lettering was produced in aluminium. The progressive numbers of the steam locomotives carried on from those of Fox Walker but the diesels were numbered in a new series commencing at 5000.

Engraved   Brass   12⁷/₈" x 10"

(29)

Engraved   Brass   10³/₄" x 7¹/₄"

Engraved   Brass   11¹/₂" x 8¹/₄"

Raised   Brass   7¹/₂" x 5¹/₄"

Engraved   Brass   11³/₄" x 8¹/₈"

Engraved   Brass   14³/₄" x 8¹/₈"

Raised   Aluminium   13¹/₄" x 8"

Raised   Brass   7¹/₄" x 5"

RFS ENGINEERING LIMITED
Kilnhurst Locomotive Works, Kilnhurst

RFS Engineering Limited (Rail Freight Services) was a subsidiary of RFS Industries Limited which was formed in 1987 following the privatisation of British Rail Engineering Limited at Doncaster. The business of Thomas Hill (Rotherham) Limited was acquired in July 1989 to produce and maintain locomotives for industry, and at the beginning of 1992 this operation was retitled RFS Locomotives. However, it was to be short lived as the works was closed by the middle of May 1993, and all business was transferred to their Doncaster site. At the end of 1993 the company called in the receivers, but fortunately was subsequently acquired by Bombardier Prorail Limited, of Horbury, near Wakefield.

During their time at Kilnhurst, RFS built five locomotives, but it has been established that none actually carried builders' plates. It appears, therefore, that the plate illustrated represents an abortive attempt by the company to introduce such plates. The plate was obtained from RFS in early 1992 and was said to be a builders' plate as 'normally fitted in the cab and painted in RFS dark blue'. Note the continued use of the Thomas Hill series of progressive numbers.

Raised   Brass   8⁵/₈" x 5³/₄"

RAILWAY MINE & PLANTATION EQUIPMENT LIMITED

Imperial House, London EC2

Railway Mine & Plantation Equipment Limited are suppliers of light and main line railway equipment and at the time of writing operate from offices at 4/5 Grosvenor Place, London SW1X 7DG. The plate depicted carries a Baguley builder's number.

| Raised | Brass | 8" x 3³/₄" |

RANSOMES & RAPIER LTD

Waterside Works, Ipswich

Ransomes was formed in 1868 to carry on a business in the supply of railway material and produced such diverse items as trackwork, portable and stationary engines and steam cranes. The first locomotives were built in 1876 for China. These were three small narrow gauge machines, one being an 0-4-0ST and the other two 0-4-2Ts. No further construction seems to have taken place after 1881 until the 1930s, when a few industrial diesels emerged.

| Engraved | Brass | 4¹/₂" x 3" |

THE RAVENGLASS & ESKDALE RAILWAY COMPANY LIMITED

Ravenglass

Originally this was a 3'0" gauge railway which operated freight services between May 1875 and April 1913 and passenger services between November 1876 and November 1908. Between August 1915 and April 1917 it was reopened in various stages as a 1'3" gauge line but the original terminus at Boot was abandoned the following year and trains operated to a temporary terminus at Dalegarth Cottages. The present station at Dalegarth was opened in 1926. The line was purchased by the present company from the Keswick Granite Company Limited in 1960.

The workshops at Ravenglass have carried out a number of major reconstructions together with new build works. This activity can be divided into two distinct periods, from 1927 to 1928 and from 1976 onwards. In the first of these a diesel locomotive was built and two steam locomotives were reconstructed. In 1976 the first new steam locomotive was built from scratch and further examples followed in 1985, 1990 and 1992. During this time work was also undertaken on a steam rebuild and two new diesels left the shops. It should be noted that not all their locomotives were fitted with builders' plates.

| Raised | Brass | 8¹/₈" x 5" |

R. & E. R.
BUILT RAVENGLASS
1980

| Engraved | Brass | 5" x 3¹/₂" |

RAILWAY MOBILE WORKSHOP No.11

Royal Engineers, Mulheim

The mobile workshop trains consisted of two machinery vans, one generator van, one welding and heavy metalwork van, a compressor van and a stores van and could be quickly deployed in theatres of war to get things moving when a railway system was taken over before the full Railway Workshop Companies were committed. They were also used to bolster up existing workshop facilities where necessary. Obviously No.11 Workshop had managed to acquire a furnace and were thus able to produce these plates. It is believed the example illustrated came from a WD 2-8-0.

| Raised | Aluminium | 10¹/₈" x 6¹/₈" |

RIDLEY SHAW & COMPANY LIMITED

Middlesbrough

Thomas Ridley undertook repairs to industrial locomotives but, for about twenty-five years, commencing in 1899, constructed half a dozen or so 0-4-0STs. It seems likely, however, that these machines were built incorporating parts of other locomotives and were not entirely of new manufacture. The 1913 plate shown is believed to be from a rebuilt Andrew Barclay locomotive. The 1936 rebuild plate is from Manning Wardle 1795 which was originally built in 1912.

| Raised | Brass | 14" x 10⁷/₈" |

| Raised | Brass | 11¹/₂" x 7¹/₂" |

RUSTON & HORNSBY LIMITED

Anchor Street, Boultham
and Iron Works, Lincoln

In 1918 the firms of Ruston, Proctor & Company Limited of Lincoln and Richard Hornsby & Sons Limited of Grantham combined, to become Ruston & Hornsby Limited. They were general engineers, but branched out into locomotive building, their first diesel being produced in 1931. Their locomotives were of various sizes and gauges and were generally very successful. However, the growth of road transport by the 1960s saw the demise of many narrow gauge industrial railways and this, combined with increasing competition for a diminishing market, led to the decision to stop building, the last loco leaving the shops in February 1969.

The Ruston & Hornsby builders' plates were fitted in the locomotives' cabs and were produced for Ruston's by a supplier in Birmingham. As locomotive production was only part of the firm's business, the progressive numbers were included with other items instead of using a separate series. These were mainly allocated in blocks, reflecting the size of particular lots under construction. Towards the end, however, an entirely new system of numbering was introduced which gave the code for the particular class of locomotive, the four-weekly period in which it was estimated it would be produced and the serial number for the period. Very few were to carry plates incorporating the new numbering system. Basically five patterns of plates seem to have been used but amongst these were numerous variations regarding the detail shown thereon.

Raised   Brass   8" x 4½"

Raised   Brass   5⅝" x 3⅛"

Raised   Brass   5¾" x 3¼"

Raised   Brass   5¾" x 3¼"

Raised   Plastic   4" x 2½"

Raised   Brass   5¾" x 3¼"

Raised   Brass   5¾" x 3¼"

Raised   Brass   5¾" x 3¼"

Engraved   Brass   5⅝" x 3⅛"

Engraved   Brass   5⅝" x 3⅛"

Engraved   Brass   5⅝" x 3⅛"

ROLLS-ROYCE LTD
Sentinel Works, Shrewsbury

Rolls-Royce Limited obtained a controlling interest in Sentinel (Shrewsbury) Limited in 1963 and continued to produce their successful range of diesel-hydraulic locomotives. Gradually, however, they transferred the locomotive business to their subsidiary Thomas Hill at Kilnhurst and this was achieved by 1971. The Sentinel Works then concentrated on the production of oil engines.

Raised   Aluminium   7¼" x 3½"

THE SENTINEL WAGGON WORKS LIMITED
Shrewsbury and Chester

In 1906 Sentinel commenced production of their first steam units but in general these were for road vehicles and It was not until 1923 that they were applied by the Company to rail traction in the form of a Sentinel-Cammell railcar and a shunting engine. It should be noted that in the previous year, Manning Wardle 0-4-0ST No.1091/1888, which worked at Lloyds Ironstone Company Limited's quarry at Isham in Northants, had been rebuilt with a vertical boiler from a Sentinel lorry by Blackwell's of Northampton under the supervision of Mr Willans, their engineer, and this machine should perhaps be regarded as the precursor of the Sentinel steam shunter. It is interesting to relate that Mr Willans later went to work for Sentinels. In the early days of their railway business many locomotives were exported. By far the biggest customer in this country was the LNER, which bought over fifty shunters and introduced a considerable number of railcars. It is estimated that some 850 steam locomotives were built, the last being in 1957.

A successful range of diesel hydraulic shunting locomotives was then developed, the first of which was ex-works in 1959. The Company was acquired by Rolls-Royce Limited in 1963, who continued to produce Sentinel diesels, eventually under their own title, until the building side of the business was transferred to Thomas Hill (Rotherham) Limited. The above relates to the firm's operation at Shrewsbury. Mention must be made of the business carried out at Chester. This was nominally a separate company and the locomotives which were rebuilt from conventional locomotives or built as new under this arrangement, carried plates with the title Sentinel Waggon Works (1920) Limited. About thirty were involved and in some cases their progressive numbers, which were within the main Sentinel range, were suffixed with CH to denote Chester. This enterprise lasted for a short period from 1924 to 1927.

Sentinel appear to have used rectangular plates of two basic styles. The early examples were most attractive, having a rounded top and depicting a logo of a knight in armour holding a sword. On both sides of this motif were listed the various patent numbers. Unusually, Sentinel plates were lettered in lower case.

Raised   Brass   5¹⁄₈" x 9⁷⁄₈"

Raised   Brass   5¹⁄₈" x 9⁷⁄₈"

Raised   Brass   5¹⁄₈" x 4"

Raised   Brass   5¹⁄₈" x 4"

D. & G. SIMS
Ruswarp, near Whitby

Mr Doug Sims started building miniature steam locomotives in 1982, and up until mid-1994 had built one of 5" gauge, which was subsequently sold, and four of 7¹⁄₄" gauge. The latest was completed during the winter of 1993/4. During the spring and summer months he operates the 7¹⁄₄" gauge Ruswarp Miniature Railway.

Raised   Brass   4⁷⁄₈" x 3⁵⁄₈"

SEVERN LAMB LIMITED
Stratford-upon-Avon

The company was founded in 1948 and was incorporated in 1956. The first locomotive built was of 7¹⁄₄" gauge and was completed in 1948/49. Unfortunately the firm's records were destroyed In a fire but In the early 1960s It appears that perhaps as many as twenty locomotives of 3¹⁄₂" and 5" gauge were built for museums and private collectors. During that decade numerous renovations, rebuilds and completions of part built locomotives also took place. The first larger gauge scratch-built locomotive was a 10¹⁄₄" 'Rio Grande' type which was constructed in 1970 for Drayton Manor Park and since then the firm have built a number of machines up to 2'0", gauge generally for the leisure industry. These have been mainly diesel or petrol locomotives but have included a few steam and electric designs.

Several types of cast and stamped plates have been utilised but the company have never kept a record of works numbers preferring to trace locomotives through clients' names or job numbers. Post 1975 the plates have reflected the month and year of manufacture but from the mid-1980s the job number has also been included.

Raised   Brass   4¹⁄₈" x 2⁵⁄₈"

⑧

Raised   Brass   4¹⁄₄" x 3"

SHARP, STEWART & COMPANY LIMITED

Atlas Works Manchester and Glasgow

Originating in Manchester Sharp Stewart & Company had a long tradition stretching back beyond the birth of the steam locomotive. The family were originally joiners and builders, but Thomas Sharp started an iron business and by 1811 was trading as Sharp Greenleaves & Company with premises in New York Street and a warehouse at Oxford Street Wharf. The firm then became known as Sharp Brothers, but soon changed its title yet again to Sharp Roberts & Company when, in about 1822, Richard Roberts became a partner. Roberts was an outstanding inventor and his talents were put to good use. The firm was mainly involved in providing machines for the cotton industry and in 1825 Roberts was responsible for evolving a mechanical mule. Unfortunately the cotton workers saw this invention as a threat to their livelihood and were so infuriated that they burnt the firms workshops to the ground. Out of the ashes, however, rose an even stronger company, which expanded and constructed the famous Atlas Works in Greater Bridgewater Street. They became interested in locomotive building and the first left the workshops in 1833. In 1843 Roberts left the company and it reverted to Sharp Brothers, but in 1852, when John Sharp retired and Charles Stewart took his place, it became Sharp Stewart & Company.

The firm became well established locomotive builders so much so that by the late 1880s they needed desperately to expand to meet demand. As fortune would have it the ill-fated Clyde Locomotive Works in Glasgow, which had been founded in 1884 by Walter Neilson in a bid to re-establish himself in the locomotive trade, came on the market and Sharp Stewart decided to move north. The Clyde Locomotive Works was renamed Atlas Works, thus retaining the link with their famous factory in Manchester. In 1903 the Company became part of the North British Locomotive Company, having built more than 5000 locomotives.

It appears that from 1852 to circa 1884 Sharp Stewart's standard plate was a large oval engraved plate but from there onwards until about 1893 they adopted a plate of similar size and design with raised lettering. This was then replaced by a smaller version with raised lettering which was used during their remaining years.

Raised	Brass	15³/₈" x 7⁵/₈"

Engraved

Raised	Brass	15³/₄" x 8"

Raised	Brass	15³/₄" x 8"

SHARP, STEWART & Cᵒ
LIMITED
ATLAS WORKS,
Nᵒ 2254 — 1872
MANCHESTER

Raised	Brass	9¹/₈" x 5⁵/₈"

Raised	Brass	8" x 4⁵/₈"

Raised	Brass	9³/₄" x 6"

WILLIAM SPENCE

Cork Street Foundry and Engineering Works, Dublin

This company produced 18 1'10" gauge locomotives between 1887 and 1921 for Arthur Guinness & Company Limited, St. James' Gate Brewery, Dublin. They were unusual machines, designed by Mr Samuel Geoghegan, the Brewery's engineer, having their cylinders and crankshaft placed horizontally over the boiler. In addition there was a unique arrangement whereby they could be mounted on broad gauge haulage wagons for use on the 5'3" gauge. Four of these wagons were built between 1888 and 1903 by Spence. Both the locomotives and wagons carried similar plates, but these differed slightly in that the latter incorporated the word 'Design' instead of 'Patent'.

Raised	Cast Iron	14¹/₂" x 8⁵/₈"

WILLIAM. SPENCE
S. GEOGHEGANS
PATENT
1895 DUBLIN 1895

Raised	Cast Iron	14¹/₂" x 8⁵/₈"

ROBERT STEPHENSON & HAWTHORNS LIMITED

Darlington, and Forth Banks Works, Newcastle-on-Tyne

In 1823 the Stephensons, in partnership with Edward Pease and Michael Longridge, established the first purpose-built workshops for the construction of railway locomotives. The first locomotive to be built was 'Locomotion' for the Stockton & Darlington Railway, and many more famous early engines followed, such as 'Rocket', 'Invicta' and 'North Star'.

Within a little over thirty years the 1000th locomotive had left the works, and by the end of the century the premises had become so cramped that it was decided that if the firm was to compete it would need to move to better accommodation. Thus land was acquired at Darlington on which a new factory was built and completed in 1902. Part of the old workshops was taken over by R. & W. Hawthorn Leslie & Company Limited, but things sometimes have a habit of turning full circle and they, in fact, came back under the wing of Stephenson's in 1937, when the locomotive side of Hawthorn Leslie's business was purchased by them for the sum of £40,260. Up to the time of this amalgamation almost 4200 locomotives had been produced, which was quite a creditable performance.

In general the new Company of Robert Stephenson & Hawthorns Limited concentrated on the production of mainline locomotives at Darlington and industrial types at Newcastle, and the first engine produced was given the progressive No.6939, which was arrived at by adding together the totals produced by both the constituent firms. In the 1940s the company became closely associated with The Vulcan Foundry and subsequently fell into the net of the English Electric Company Limited.

The last conventional steam engine was built in 1958, but a fireless locomotive completed early the following year brought the curtain down on steam production. In 1960 the Forth Banks Works at Newcastle was closed and at the beginning of 1962 the works at Darlington was retitled the English Electric Company Limited, Stephenson Works, thereby finally fully integrating the firm into that group. All was not well, however, as the locomotive industry was in decline and it was perhaps no surprise when in 1964 the works was closed, thus ending a direct link with one of the most famous of the pioneer railwaymen.

| Engraved | Brass | 9" x 5" |

| Raised | Brass | 9⅝" x 6⅛" |

| Engraved | Brass | 10¼" x 6⅝" |

| Engraved | Brass | 11¼" x 5¼" |

| Raised | Brass | 11⅛" x 5⅛" |

| Engraved | Brass | 11¼" x 5¼" |

| Engraved | Brass | 11¼" x 5¼" |

| Engraved | Brass | 13½" x 8" |

| Engraved | Brass | 11¼" x 5¼" |

| Engraved | Brass | 11¼" x 5¼" |

| Engraved | Brass | 11" x 6½" |

| Engraved | Brass | 11¼" x 5¼" |

| Engraved | Brass | 8¾" x 4⅞" |

30
63

Engraved Brass $11\frac{1}{4}$" x $5\frac{1}{4}$"

31
00

Engraved Brass $11\frac{3}{8}$" x $5\frac{3}{8}$"

Raised Brass $12\frac{7}{8}$" x $8\frac{1}{2}$"

Raised Brass 13" x $8\frac{5}{8}$"

32

Raised Brass $12\frac{7}{8}$" x $8\frac{1}{2}$"

63

Raised Brass 13" x $8\frac{1}{2}$"

33

Raised Brass $12\frac{3}{4}$" x $8\frac{1}{2}$"

Raised Brass 6" x 4"

Engraved Brass $11\frac{3}{8}$" x $5\frac{3}{8}$"

34

Raised Brass 12" x $5\frac{3}{8}$"

Raised Brass 13" x $8\frac{5}{8}$"

Raised Brass 8" x $5\frac{1}{8}$"

Raised Brass 13" x $8\frac{5}{8}$"

STRACHAN & HENSHAW LIMITED
Bristol

Between 1966 and the early 1970s Strachan & Henshaw constructed, under licence from the Whiting Corporation of Illinois, thirteen 'Trackmobiles', all but one being for the home market. These machines were capable of working on both road and rail, weighed $4\frac{1}{2}$ tons each and had a maximum speed of 12 mph.

The plate to which the authors have access is unfortunately in too poor a condition to be photographed or for a rubbing to be taken from it. It appears originally to have had white lettering printed on a dark green background. The locomotives details are stamped into the plate. The layout of the plate is as follows:

Printed Aluminium $6\frac{1}{2}$" x $3\frac{1}{4}$"

53

TMA ENGINEERING LIMITED
Birmingham

TMA Engineering was formed in 1973, primarily concerned with the service and repair of industrial power presses. However, in 1978 at the request of the Romney, Hythe & Dymchurch Railway they overhauled a steam locomotive frame, and this led to three more steam locomotives being overhauled for that railway. In the 1980s two diesel hydraulic locomotives were designed and built for the RH&DR and two others went to a customer in Japan. The firm has also designed, repaired and constructed a number of steam locomotives of various gauges.

TMA allocate progressive numbers to any job, be it a clutch key for a press or a complete locomotive. These numbers now exceed 18,000.

TMA ENGINEERING LTD
BUILT 1983
WORKS Nº 6143
BIRMINGHAM ENGLAND

Raised   Brass   7" x 4¼"

Raised   Brass   5¾" x 3⅛"

Raised   Brass   7¾" x 5"

UNILOKOMOTIVE LTD INTERNATIONAL DIVISION
Mervue Industrial Estate, Galway

Hugo Aeckerle & Company, Hamburg, Germany, use the trade name Unilok for the machines they produce which are capable of working on either road or rail. A number of these were constructed under licence by Engineering Products Limited, Frances Street, Dublin, until circa 1972 and thereafter at Unilokomotive Limited in Galway.

On the plate illustrated is attached what appears to be a rubberised strip, into which the type of the machine has been embossed. In addition, the plate is accompanied by a separate metal strip into which is stamped 'TYPE 6000S Nº 1997'.

Printed   Plastic   4⅝" x 2⅜"

THE VULCAN FOUNDRY LIMITED
Newton-le-Willows

The Vulcan Foundry was established in 1830, in the wake of the euphoria surrounding the opening of the Liverpool & Manchester Railway, with a view to supplying all kinds of general engineering paraphernalia to this infant industry, particularly in that part of the world. It was founded by Charles Tayleur, who, besides being a merchant, was a director of the Liverpool & Manchester Railway, and it first went under the title of Tayleur & Company. In 1832 Robert Stephenson joined him in this venture, but this appears to have only been a short-lived relationship. The first locomotives were built in 1833, being two 0-4-0s for the North Union Railway, appropriately named 'Tayleur' and 'Stephenson'. Before the decade was out the business was not only producing for the home market but exporting locomotives overseas, examples going to Austria, America, Belgium, France and Russia. In 1847 the firm adopted the title The Vulcan Foundry Company and in 1864 became The Vulcan Foundry Company Limited, changing yet again in 1898 to The Vulcan Foundry Limited. Many different types of steam locomotives were built over the years and when steam production ceased early in 1955 over 6000 had left the shops. The factory was reorganised to tackle diesel and electric traction and also became part of The English Electric Company. In 1962 it was retitled The English Electric Company Limited, Vulcan Works.

Raised   Brass   9⅝" x 5⅝"

Raised   Brass   9¾" x 5¾"

Raised   Brass   9½" x 5⅜"

(35)

Raised   Brass   9½" x 5⅜"

(35)

Raised   Brass   10⅜" x 5⅞"

Raised Brass 9" x 5¼"

⑫

Raised Brass 5½" x 2½"

Raised Brass 9¾" x 5¾"

⑱

Raised Brass 13⅛" x 5⅜"

⑱

Raised Brass 9" x 5"

⑱

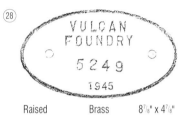

Raised Brass 8⅞" x 4⅞"

Raised Brass 9¾" x 5"

JOHN F. WAKE
Geneva Engineering Works, Darlington

The sale of locomotives often took place through dealers such as John F. Wake and sometimes they fitted their own plates either in addition to, or in place of the original builders plates. In some cases the reason for this, no doubt, was to try and secure any future orders for spares. The plate shown was from a locomotive originally built by Black, Hawthorn & Company of Gateshead, in 1876.

Raised Brass 12" x 8"

WIGAN COAL & IRON COMPANY LIMITED
Kirkless, Wigan

Between 1865 and 1912 this company built three 0-4-0ST and fifteen 0-6-0STs in their workshops, for use in various local collieries.

Raised Brass 15" x 6¾"

E. B. WILSON & CO
Railway Foundry, Leeds

The Railway Foundry was set up in 1838 by Shepherd & Todd and traded under that title until 1846, when it was taken over by Fenton Craven & Company. This partnership was to last for barely a year, as at the end of 1846 the firm was acquired by Mr E. B. Wilson and became E. B. Wilson & Company. The Railway Foundry soon acquired a reputation for quality workmanship and was at the forefront in its field, but the shareholders were unhappy with the way in which Wilson ran the business, and in 1856 matters came to a head and Wilson left. Subsequently action in Chancery was taken in 1858 and the company was closed down, a sad demise for an enterprise which had the makings of a major force in locomotive building. The ghost of the Railway Foundry lived on, however, for the embryonic Manning Wardle & Company built many of their early locomotives to Wilson's designs and Hudswell & Clarke having purchased part of the site to set up their business, adopted the name for their works.

Raised Brass 21½" x 6"

Engraved Brass 21½" x 6"

WINGROVE & ROGERS LIMITED

Kirkby, Liverpool

Wingrove & Rogers commenced the construction of battery electric locomotives in the mid 1920s, carrying on the business of British Electric Vehicles Limited, and continued to build these machines until fairly recent times.

In July 1988 the business was acquired by Pikrose & Company Limited, Delta Works, Audenshaw, Manchester, who by early 1994 had constructed at least 60 locomotives. At first they continued Wingrove's series of progressive numbers, but after about 18 months introduced their own system. This was changed again in 1992 and now comprises a prefix letter to indicate the year of manufacture, the job number and a suffix showing the locomotive's serial number within the job lot.

| Engraved | Brass | 3⁷/₈" x 4¹/₈" |

⑧

| Engraved/Raised | Brass | 4¹/₂" x 3¹/₄" |

| Raised | Brass | 4" x 6" |

HUGH WOOD & COMPANY LIMITED

Gateshead-on-Tyne

This firm were mining specialist and in September 1944 came to an agreement with Hudswell Clarke & Company Limited regarding the manufacture of flame-proofed diesel mines locomotives. Under this arrangement they acted as sole selling agents, the machines being marketed under the Huwood-Hudswell banner. Some, at least, carried their plates.

| Raised | Brass | 9¹/₄" x 4⁷/₈" |

| Raised | Brass | 5" x 3" |

YORKSHIRE ENGINE COMPANY LIMITED

Meadow-Hall Works, Sheffield

The Yorkshire Engine Company was established in 1865 and in addition to locomotives also manufactured items for the mining industry. Their output comprised both main line and industrial types for both home and abroad and interestingly a considerable number of Fairlies were produced during the period from the early 1870s to the end of the first decade of this century. In 1930 and again in 1949 orders were received for 0-6-0 PTs for the GWR and the Western Region, the last being completed in 1956 (B.R. No.3409); this machine had the distinction of being the final steam locomotive produced by the firm. After this, work comprised diesel locomotives mainly for industrial users. In 1948 the United Steel Companies took over the business and in the firm's centenary year it changed hands again and was acquired by Rolls-Royce Limited who soon transferred the work to their factory at Shrewsbury (the former Sentinel Works).

The progressive numbers of this firm are a classic example of how to confuse the unsuspecting, as although in the early days a continuous run of numbers was used, from the early 1880s onwards many other items produced were included within the series, giving the impression that lots more locomotives had been built than really existed. This can be illustrated by the fact that the last steam locomotive constructed carried the progressive No.2584 whereas in reality fewer than 800 locomotives had left their shops.

In the main, oval plates were used but some of the diesels were also fitted with an additional large rectangular aluminium builders' plate giving details of the equipment suppliers.

| Raised | Brass | 12¹/₂" x 7¹/₈" |

Raised   Brass   12³/₄" x 7³/₈"

Raised   Brass   6" x 4"

Raised   Brass   11" x 6"

Raised   Brass   12³/₄" x 7³/₈"

(63)

Raised   Brass   11" x 6"

(63)

Raised   Brass   11" x 6"

Raised   Aluminium   17¹/₈" x 7³/₈"

Raised   Aluminium   17¹/₈" x 7³/₈"

YORKSHIRE ENGINE
COMPANY LIMITED
Rotherham

The new Yorkshire Engine Company Limited was formed late 1988 by ex Thomas Hill personnel and is primarily concerned with locomotives, but is also involved with training, electronic engine monitoring and permanent way equipment. At the time of publication YECL had not built a completely new locomotive, but had undertaken several major repairs and rebuilds on locomotives and railcars and occasionally worked in conjunction with ABB Transportation at Crewe Works.

All locomotive contracts are given a three figure number prefixed by a letter 'L', but not all locomotives carry plates. Earlier plates did not carry the word 'REWORKED' and any new construction in the future will also have the word deleted.

(8)

Raised   Brass   7" x 4¹/₂"

STOP PRESS

Previously unknown plates or variations of plates are always likely to turn up.
Information on the following plates came to hand too late to be included on the appropriate page
under their respective heading, but are included here, for the interest of readers.

E. E. BAGULEY LIMITED
(addition to main entry on page 12)

Raised   Brass   7¼" x 4¾"

THE BRUSH ELECTRICAL ENGINEERING CO LTD
(addition to main entry on page 20)

Raised/Engraved   Aluminium   9⅞" x 5¾"

MOTOR RAIL LIMITED
(additions to main entry on page 43)

Printed   Aluminium   6" x 3"

Printed   Aluminium   6" x 3"

MUIR HILL ENGINEERING LIMITED
(addition to main entry on page 43)

Raised   Cast Iron   10⅞" x 5¼"

BLACK, HAWTHORN & COMPANY
(addition to main entry on page 19)

Raised   Brass   15¾" x 10"

MANNING WARDLE & COMPANY LIMITED
(addition to main entry on page 40)

Raised   Brass   10⅞" x 6⅛"

PART TWO

RAILWAY COMPANY
WORKSHOPS

In the very early days of railways, motive power was purchased from private builders, but as their systems expanded most of the larger companies set up workshops to design and construct locomotives for their own requirements. This contrasted sharply with the practice in many other countries, where locomotives continued to be ordered in large quantities from private builders. The Great Western Railway and the London & North Western Railway in particular became almost self-sufficient, and this state of affairs did not go without some criticism from the private sector who saw the situation as being one of unfair competition, particularly when the L&NWR began to supply locomotives for the use of the Lancashire & Yorkshire Railway. They sought and obtained an injunction against the L&NWR and the practice had to cease, but it did not prevent the railway companies, on occasion, buying locomotives that were already in service on other railways. The private builders had, therefore, to content themselves with supplying main line locomotives within this constriction, to industry and, of course, to the world markets.

Photograph above: *Inside the former Highland Railway Lochgorm Works, Inverness, Caledonian '812' class 0-6-0 No.57587 receives attention to the centre pair of driving wheels. The shop also includes four LMS Class 5MT 4-6-0s Nos 44801, 44992, 45320 and 45309.* Roger Shenton, 29th June 1954.

RAILWAY COMPANY WORKSHOPS

The following is a list of the principal railway company workshops, together with the dates during which the construction of both steam and non-steam locomotives took place and the name of the last pre-grouping company to own these workshops.

Workshop	Period of Loco Construction	Last Pre-Grouping Company
Ashford	1849 - 1952	South Eastern & Chatham
Belfast (Gt Victoria St)	1867 - 1882	Great Northern of Ireland
Belfast (York Road)	1870 - 1942	Northern Counties Committee
Brighton	1852 - 1957	London, Brighton & South Coast
Cardiff	1856 - 1897	Taff Vale
Crewe	1845 - 1991	London & North Western
Darlington	1864 - 1964	North Eastern
Derby	1851 - 1977	Midland
Doncaster	1867 - 1987	Great Northern
Dublin (Broadstone)	1879 - 1927	Midland & Great Western of Ireland
Dublin (Grand Canal St)	1851 - 1911	Dublin & South Eastern
Dublin (Inchicore)	1852 - 1963	Great Southern & Western
Dundalk	1887 - 1937	Great Northern of Ireland
Eastleigh	1910 - 1962	London & South Western
Edinburgh (St. Margarets)	1856 - 1869	North British
Gateshead	1849 - 1910	North Eastern
Glasgow (Cowlairs)	1844 - 1924	North British
Glasgow (St. Rollox)	1854 - 1928	Caledonian
Greenock	1846 - 1855	Caledonian
Horwich	1889 - 1962	Lancashire & Yorkshire
Inverness (Lochgorm)	1869 - 1906	Highland
Inverurie	1909 - 1921	Great North of Scotland
Kilmarnock	1857 - 1921	Glasgow & South Western
London (Bow)	1863 - 1910	North London
London (Longhedge)	1869 - 1904	London, Chatham & Dover
London (Neasden)	1896 - 1898	Metropolitan
London (Nine Elms)	1843 - 1908	London & South Western
London (Stratford)	1851 - 1924	Great Eastern
Manchester (Gorton)	1858 - 1954	Great Central
Manchester (Miles Platting)	1847 - 1881	Lancashire & Yorkshire
Melton Constable	1897 - 1910	Midland & Great Northern Joint
Stoke	1868 - 1923	North Staffordshire
Swindon	1846 - 1979	Great Western
Wolverton	1845 - 1863	London & North Western
Wolverhampton	1859 - 1906	Great Western
York	1854 - 1884	North Eastern

As can be gleaned from the table, in mainland Britain by the time of the Grouping in 1923 there were fourteen company workshops producing new locomotives, but by the end of that decade this figure had been reduced to ten. All of these continued into British Railways' days, but by the 1980s solely Crewe and Doncaster were actively engaged in construction. Today only Crewe alone may have the necessary capacity, but it seems that if present trends continue it is unlikely that further locomotive construction will take place there. In Ireland the railway workshops sadly reached the position of offering only repair facilities many years ago and Inchicore and York Road no longer build new locomotives. In practice the wheel has almost turned full circle back to the early days of railways and the private builder has once more come to the fore as the main supplier.

In general, builders' plates from the pre-grouping companies are few and far between, with the exception of the Great Northern Railway and Great Central Railway and even these are not too plentiful. There are various reasons for this. Collecting only became fashionable to any degree after the Second World War so many early plates were lost through lack of interest. The railway companies themselves also did not help matters. In the case of the Great Western it was decided around 1911 to discontinue the practice of fitting builders' plates to newly constructed locomotives and also to remove them from those engines already in stock. After the Grouping the LM&SR adopted a policy of replacing the plates on their constituents' locomotives with their own standard design and these were also fitted to new locomotives. Some pre-grouping

companies incorporated building details into number plates which disappeared when the 'Big Four' introduced their new numbering schemes and the London & North Western Railway also used their nameplates for this purpose. Some companies of course, never fitted builders' plates at all.

After the grouping, Crewe, Derby, Horwich, St. Rollox and Stoke used the standard LMS plates based on the Midland Railway pattern. Ashford, Brighton, Eastleigh and Swindon utilised a version of this style of plate on the Stanier Class 8F 2-8-0s which they constructed during the Second World War, but otherwise did not fit plates. The L&NER workshops at Cowlairs, Gateshead, Gorton, Inverurie and Stratford all fitted standard L&NER 9" x 5" plates to their locomotives, most of which had been built by the former pre-grouping companies. Darlington and Doncaster however, in addition to fitting the 9" x 5" plates also chose to follow the tradition of the Great Northern Railway by emulating their brass, oval engraved style of plate. Darlington did not start fitting these plates until 1943 and Doncaster deviated by using cast iron oval plates with raised lettering for the Stanier Class 8F 2-8-0 locomotives.

Under British Railways the position can be summarised as follows:

Ashford appear to have fitted plates only to diesel locomotive No.10201, presumably because this locomotive was selected for display at the Festival of Britain in 1951. The plates were rectangular, brass and had raised lettering.

Brighton used only the standard oval plates which were introduced by British Railways and which owed an obvious ancestry to those of the LM&SR. These simply gave the name of the workshop and date of construction.

Crewe also used the standard oval plates together with standard larger rectangular plates cast in aluminium. The latter plates were used on certain main line diesel locomotives and additionally gave details of the power equipment for the locomotive concerned. In 1966-67 Crewe workshops rebuilt ten Class 71 Bo-Bo electric locomotives to Class 74 and fitted these with oval, chromed brass plates which also gave information relating to the power equipment.

Darlington at first used an oval engraved brass plate inscribed

'NORTH EASTERN REGION' instead of 'LONDON NORTH EASTERN RAILWAY', but this was very short-lived and a plainer engraved brass plate showing only the progressive number, the name of the workshop and the year of construction was quickly introduced. The Standard classes of steam locomotives and diesel electric shunters produced at Darlington however, carried the LM&SR style plates whilst main line diesel locomotives were fitted with the rectangular aluminium plates giving the power equipment information.

Derby built locomotives, with one exception, carried the standard BR oval plate or the rectangular aluminium pattern. The Fell diesel mechanical locomotive No 10100 was fitted with an oval brass plate, with raised lettering and power equipment details.

Doncaster continued to use engraved brass plates that showed only the progressive number, the name of the workshop and the date of build. The Standard steam classes and diesel shunters, however, were fitted with the standard oval pattern plate. The Class AL5 and AL6 Bo-Bo electric locomotives were given rectangular aluminium plates with power equipment supplier shown, but these plates were much smaller than the standard pattern used by Crewe, Darlington and Derby. Finally, the Bo-Bo electric locomotives (later Class 71) had oval, chromed brass plates similar to those fitted by Crewe to the ten locomotives converted to Class 74.

Eastleigh built six Bo-Bo electro-diesels in 1962 (Class 73/0) and fitted these locomotives with oval, chrome plated brass plates, which also gave the power equipment supplier information. Some of these plates are known to be made in fibreglass, and are thought to be early replacements.

Gorton reintroduced builders plates for the construction of the Class EM1 and EM2 Bo-Bo and Co-Co electric locomotives. These plates were very similar to the Darlington and Doncaster engraved oval brass plates which showed the progressive number, the workshop and date of construction. In addition, at least one of the L&NER Class B1 4-6-0 engines built in 1949 carried a L&NER 9" x 5" plate which instead of the locomotive's running number, showed the Gorton Works progressive number, and so can rightly be held as a builders' plate proper.

Horwich used only the standard oval plates.

Swindon, like Horwich only used the standard oval plate.

The standard oval plates introduced by British Railways were made of aluminium, brass, cast iron or fibreglass. On some of these plates the dates were engraved. A summary of the materials used by the various workshops in the manufacture of these plates is as follows:

	Aluminium	Brass	Cast Iron	Fibreglass
Brighton		•	•	
Crewe	•		•	
Darlington		•	•	•
Derby	•	•	•	•
Doncaster			•	•
Horwich			•	•
Swindon	•	•	•	

Under the provisions of the 1968 Transport Act the railway workshops were given a separate identity, becoming British Rail Engineering Limited and were able to compete for work against the rest of the private sector. With one exception new construction was concentrated at Crewe and Doncaster and the Class 56 and 58 diesel electric locomotives built there were fitted with small rectangular aluminium plates with raised lettering simply stating the name of the company, the workshop and date of construction. On the Class 90 electric locomotives built at Crewe, a much larger and more elaborate aluminium oval plate incorporating the BREL logo was used on the initial batch but on those built later the company reverted to a plainer and more austere oval plate, of which, two variations are known to be carried by these locomotives. Undoubtedly the most unusual task undertaken by British Rail Engineering Limited, was the construction at Swindon of twenty 0-8-0 metre gauge diesel hydraulic shunters for Kenya Railways. These were part of an order sub-contracted by Hunslet Holdings Plc and the locomotives were fitted with oval brass builders' plates echoing Hunslet's style and carrying that firm's progressive number, but showing they were supplied by BRE-Metro Limited.

In 1987 the locomotive workshops at Doncaster, Eastleigh and Glasgow were handed back to British Rail to operate as Level 5 maintenance facilities under a newly formed company British Rail Maintenance Limited but from September 1994 came under the banner of Rail Maintenance Limited as a prelude to possible privatisation. British Rail Engineering Limited became BREL (1988) Limited in 1988 and in the summer of 1989 was retitled BREL Limited. Of the two locomotive workshops remaining under their control, Derby closed after the cessation of repair work in 1988 and on 2nd September 1992 Crewe Workshops became part of the Asea Brown Boveri Company, trading under the title of ABB Transportation Limited.

The tables and illustrations for the main line workshops now follow. The various owning companies have been ignored and each workshop is simply given alphabetically with the plates listed and pictured in order of construction. It thus forms an easy reference of the plates produced by the individual workshops in what is a logical sequence of usage. There are, however, two exceptions to this. The first is the standard LM&SR plates which were used to replace certain private builders' plates and these are listed in a section of their own after the information on the workshops. The other exception is the L&NER and BR(E) 9" x 5" plates. The authors gave much thought about including these in the work, but as they generally give details of where the locomotives were built and when, it was decided they should receive some coverage. Their history is quite involved as they often replaced both original company and private builders' plates, acted as rebuild plates or in some cases had the word 'BUILT' cast into them. Some carried the post-grouping number allocated to the locomotive and others the numbers allocated under the 1946 renumbering scheme or by British Railways. In addition they were sometimes found on tenders either carrying the same number as the locomotive to which the tender was attached or, as in the case of Darlington, a separate series of numbers for tenders only. As these plates fall readily into a category of their own and were fitted by the railway workshops they have also been included at the end of the listings for the main line workshops.

ASHFORD

The South Eastern Railway set up their workshops at Ashford in 1846 but it was 1853 before the first passenger locomotive was fully fabricated there, although even then the boiler was obtained from an outside contractor. Steam locomotive construction totalled 790, ending in 1944 with a batch of fourteen LM&SR 8F 2-8-0s.

In 1937 three 0-6-0 diesel electric shunters were built and a further 26 followed between 1949-1952, and these eventually became British Railways Class 12. In 1950 an 0-6-0 diesel mechanical locomotive was built which was intended for both shunting and branch line operation. Ashford's greatest achievements in the modern traction field must be the Co-Co electrics Nos CC1 and CC2 (later British Railways 20001 and 20002) and the 1Co-Co1 diesel electrics Nos 10201 and 10202 which left the shops in 1941, 1945, 1950 and 1951 respectively.

Following the transfer of locomotive work to Eastleigh in July 1962 the workshops took on a major role in the building, conversion and routine repair of wagons, although they did manufacture the roof sections for the British Railways Class 56 diesel electric locomotives. The end came in 1981 when a rationalisation of operations by BREL resulted in the works' closure.

Raised   Brass   9¹⁄₈" x 5¹⁄₄"

BELFAST
York Road

York Road Works in Belfast was established by the Belfast & Northern Counties Railway in 1870 and constructed six locomotives before being taken over by the Midland Railway in 1903. Under the new management the railway was retitled the Northern Counties Committee (MR) and another nine were built before Grouping in 1923 followed by a further twenty-two by the LM&SR. The last to leave the works was a Class W 2-6-0 in 1942.

BRIGHTON

Locomotives were built at Brighton between 1852 and 1957, the last being British Railways Standard Class 4 2-6-4T No. 80154 which was ex-works on 26th March 1957. During that period 1,211 steam locomotives were built plus one diesel and one electric. Undoubtedly, however, the works' most unusual project was the order in 1947 for five Bulleid designed 'Leader' class 0-6-6-OTs, only one of which was completed and actually ran trials before the whole idea was quietly dropped and the locomotive scrapped, together with the two partially constructed locomotives.

Part of the workshops were sold to BMW for the production of their Isetta cars in early 1957, although locomotive repairs continued until the end of 1958.

Engraved   Brass   16" x 9³⁄₄"

Engraved   Brass   6¹⁄₂" x 3⁷⁄₈"

Raised   Brass   11¹⁄₄" x 5⁷⁄₈"

Raised   Brass   10³⁄₄" x 6"

Engraved   Brass   6¹⁄₂" x 3⁷⁄₈"

Engraved   Brass   9⁵⁄₈" x 5⁵⁄₈"

Raised   Brass   11" x 5⁵⁄₈"

Raised   Brass   10³⁄₈" x 6"

Engraved   Brass   9³⁄₄" x 6⁷⁄₈"

Raised   Cast Iron   10¹⁄₂" x 6"

COWLAIRS

Cowlairs Works was built in 1841 in anticipation of the needs of the Edinburgh & Glasgow Railway which was to open the following year. In 1844 two locomotives were built for use on the Cowlairs Incline and approximately twenty more were constructed up until the time of the company's amalgamation with the North British Railway in July 1865. By 1924, when construction ceased, around 900 locomotives had left the shops. The works were closed in September 1966 and by early 1968 were in the process of being dismantled.

NORTH BRITISH RAILWAY
256
COWLAIRS WORKS 1913

Raised   Brass   Not known

CREWE

The works at Crewe epitomised the self-sufficiency of the major main line companies in producing their own motive power. Set up by the Grand Junction Railway in 1843, the first locomotive was produced in 1845 just one year before the company became part of the London & North Western Railway. During its existence many famous classes of locomotive emerged from the works, including the Claughtons, Experiments, Precedents and, in later years, the Princess Royals and Princess Coronations.

At its height in LM&SR days the works area covered nearly 140 acres, almost 30% of which comprised buildings, and employed over 20,000 staff. The last steam locomotive was built in 1958 giving an impressive total of 7,331. In 1957 Crewe Works built its first diesel electric 0-6-0 shunters, which were later classified as 08s, and to date non-steam production figures stand as follows:

Diesel	560
Electro-diesel	10 (rebuilds)
Electric	118
High-Speed Train Power Cars	199 (including the two prototypes)
Total	887

Since September 1992 the works has traded as a private company called ABB Transportation Limited.

Raised   Brass   10½" x 5⅞"

Raised   Cast Iron   10½" x 6"

Raised   Brass   10⅜" x 6"

Raised   Brass   10¼" x 6"

Raised   Cast Iron   10¼" x 5⅞"

Raised   Aluminium   13" x 6½"

Raised   Aluminium   13" x 6½"

Raised   Aluminium   13" x 6½"

Raised   Aluminium   13" x 6½"

Raised   Brass/Chromed   10½" x 6"

DARLINGTON

North Road Works at Darlington were established in 1863 by the Stockton & Darlington Railway as a result of the company's wish to expand its locomotive facilities which were sited at Shildon. The first locomotive left the shops in October 1864 and the final one appeared in August 1964. This was British Railways Type 2 Bo-Bo diesel electric No D7597 (later BR 25247). The total output comprised 2,269 steam locomotives, 11 electrics and 506 diesels. Closure came in April 1966.

| Raised | Aluminium | 7" x 4¾" |

| Raised | Aluminium | 9¼" x 5¼" |

| Raised | Aluminium | 9¼" x 5⅛" |

(49)

| Engraved | Brass | 12¾" x 7½" |

| Engraved | Brass | 13¼" x 7⅝" |

| Engraved | Brass | 13¼" x 7⅝" |

| Engraved | Brass | 13" x 7½" |

| Engraved | Brass | 13⅛" x 7⅝" |

| Engraved | Brass | 12⅛" x 6¼" |

| Raised | Cast Iron | 10½" x 6" |

| Raised | Aluminium | 13" x 6½" |

| Raised | Aluminium | 13" x 6½" |

(48)

| Raised | Fibreglass | 10⅜" x 6" |

DERBY

The North Midland Railway, which was incorporated into the Midland Railway in 1844, chose to build their locomotive works in Derby and these were opened in 1840. It was not, however, until 1851 that new construction began when ten single-wheelers were produced for passenger work. Steam locomotive production ceased when 5MT 4-6-0 No. 73154 was put into traffic on 14th June 1957. Sources seem to differ slightly as to the total number of steam locomotives produced, but this appears to be around 2,940.

A 4-wheeled battery electric locomotive was built on a modified wagon under-frame by the Midland Railway in 1913, for use at the West India Docks in London.

Diesel construction commenced in the early 1930s when an 0-6-0 diesel hydraulic shunter was built utilising the frames of a Midland Railway tank locomotive. Construction continued at Derby until May 1967 when the last locomotive emerged. This was a British Railways Type 2 Bo-Bo diesel electric No. D7677, which later became Class 25 25327. After that the only other new build order with which the works dealt was in 1977 for six Advanced Passenger Train Power Cars. In total Derby built just over one thousand non-steam units.

One interesting project undertaken during 1974/75 which is worthy of mention was the refurbishment of five Class 08 shunters for use by the LAMCO Mining Company in Liberia. These were fitted with plates showing that they had been modified at Derby.

Repair work ceased at Derby in 1988 and as a result the works closed.

| Raised | Brass | 10³/₈" x 5⁷/₈" |

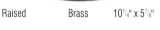

| Raised | Brass | 10¹/₄" x 5⁷/₈" |

| Raised | Brass | 10³/₈" x 6" |

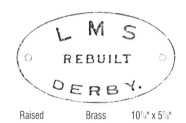

| Raised | Brass | 10¹/₄" x 5⁷/₈" |

| Raised | Brass | 10³/₈" x 6" |

(48)

| Raised | Brass | 10¹/₈" x 5³/₄" |

(48)

| Raised | Brass | 10¹/₂" x 6" |

| Raised | Brass | 10⁵/₈" x 6¹/₄" |

| Raised | Cast Iron | 10⁵/₈" x 6" |

(48)

BUILT
1955
DERBY

| Raised | Fibreglass | 10¹/₄" x 5⁷/₈" |

| Raised | Aluminium | 13" x 6¹/₂" |

| Raised | Aluminium | 13" x 6¹/₂" |

| Raised | Aluminium | 13" x 6¹/₂" |

Raised   Aluminium   13" x 6½"

Raised   Fibreglass   10" x 5⅞"

DONCASTER

As the Great North Railway rapidly expanded it became apparent that the original workshops at Boston would be unable to cope so a decision was taken to establish new premises at Doncaster. These came into operation in 1853 but the first new locomotive did not emerge from 'The Plant' as it was known, until 1867. The Stirling 'Singles', the Ivatt 'Atlantics' and the Gresley and Thompson 'Pacifics' were but a few of their excellent products. The last steam locomotive, the 2,224th, left the works in October 1957 and was British Railways Standard Class 4 2-6-0 No. 76114.

Non-steam building commenced in 1941 when the precursor of the Manchester-Sheffield-Wath electrics L&NER No. 6701, subsequently becoming BR 26000 and named 'Tommy', was built. In total Doncaster con-

structed 255 diesels and 116 electrics up until March 1987 when the last British Rail Class 58 (No 58050) heavy freight locomotive was completed. These figures include the eleven battery electric locomotives built in 1973/74 for the London Transport Executive and three diesels in 1970 in association with The Hunslet Engine Company for Northern Ireland Railways. In 1975 four Class 501 EMUs were converted to battery electric locomotives and a similar number were dealt with in 1980, but as these were not completely new build they have not been taken into account.

Currently the premises at Doncaster are used as a maintenance facility.

Raised   Brass   15¼" x 3½"

Raised   Brass   10⅝" x 6½"

Raised   Brass   12¼" x 7⅜"

Engraved   Brass   17⅜" x 9½"

Raised   Brass   10⅝" x 6½"

Engraved   Brass   12⅛" x 7¼"

(28)
(49)

Engraved   Brass   12⅛" x 7¼"

(50)

Engraved   Brass   12¼" x 7¼"

(51)

Raised   Brass   12¼" x 7⅜"

Engraved   Brass   13¼" x 7⅝"

Engraved   Brass   13¼" x 7½"

Engraved   Brass   13⅛" x 7½"

Raised   Cast Iron   13³⁄₈" x 7⁵⁄₈"

Engraved   Brass   13¼" x 7½"

Engraved   Brass   12¼" x 6³⁄₈"

Raised   Cast Iron   10½" x 6"

(48)

Raised   Fibreglass   10⅛" x 5⅞"

Raised   Brass/Chromed   10½" x 6"

Raised   Aluminium   8½" x 5¾"

Raised   Aluminium   8½" x 5¾"

Raised   Aluminium   7" x 4¾"

Raised   Aluminium   7" x 4¾"

DUNDALK

Dundalk Works of the Great Northern Railway of Ireland opened in 1882 on the former site of the old works of the Dublin & Belfast Junction Railway. It was not a very big works and the Company obtained many of its locomotives from outside contractors. Nevertheless, between 1887 and 1939 forty-seven steam locomotives were built comprising 0-6-0s, 2-4-2Ts, 4-4-0Ts and 4-4-0s.

Raised   Brass   9⅞" x 5⅞"

Raised   Brass   9⅞" x 5⅞"

Raised   Brass   9⅞" x 5⅞"

Raised   Brass   8¼" x 4⅜"

Raised   Brass   8⅜" x 4½"

GORTON

It was not until ten years after the completion of the workshops at Gorton for the Manchester, Sheffield & Lincolnshire Railway in 1848 that the first locomotive was completed and up until the formation of the Great Central Railway on 1st August 1897, nearly 500 locomotives had been constructed. By the time British Railways was formed in January 1948 that figure had almost doubled. Under British Railways there was an increasing tendency to concentrate building at Darlington and Doncaster and only ten more steam locomotives were built making a grand total of 1,007. However, the construction of the Class EM1 and EM2 electrics for the Manchester-Sheffield-Wath dc electric scheme was entrusted to the works and in total sixty-four of these machines were built between 1950-1954. After this the works continued to carry out repairs until its closure in June 1963.

Raised   Brass   6⅝" x 4⅜"

Raised   Brass   9⅞" x 5¼"

Raised   Brass   10½" x 6⅝"

Raised   Brass   12¼" x 8½"

Engraved   Brass   11⅞" x 6¼"

EASTLEIGH

As a result of their workshops at Nine Elms finding it increasingly difficult to cope, the London & South Western Railway decided to build new premises at Eastleigh and these were opened in 1910. New construction started the same year and the last steam locomotive, the 320th, was completed in 1950. From 1956 until 1961 work was undertaken on the major rebuilding of the thirty 'Merchant Navy', forty-three 'West Country' and seventeen 'Battle of Britain' Class locomotives which arguably could be regarded as new machines and therefore eligible for inclusion in the aforementioned total.

Eastleigh's only involvement with the building of non-steam traction was in 1962 when six Bo-Bo electro-diesel locomotives were produced, eventually becoming Class 73/0.

Today Eastleigh Works is in use as a maintenance facility.

Raised   Brass/Chromed   10¾" x 6⅛"

HORWICH

Because the Miles Platting Works of the Lancashire & Yorkshire Railway lacked the facility to expand, the Company decided to build new premises at Horwich and in November 1887 repair work commenced there. 1889 saw the start of new construction which continued until 1962 by which time, 1,840 steam locomotives and 169 diesels had been built, all the latter being British Railways 350hp 0-6-0 diesel electric shunters, later known as Class 08. However, in August 1912 an electric locomotive was constructed at Horwich using the frames and wheels of a 2-4-2T. It was fitted with 4 x 150hp Dick, Kerr motors. Similarly in July 1917 another electric locomotive was built which had British Thomson-Houston motors.

Following the cessation of locomotive repairs in May 1964 the works dealt with repairs to EMUs, carriages, wagons and civil engineering equipment and, as well as various conversion jobs, also undertook some wagon construction. In November 1983 work ceased and the premises were sold.

Raised   Brass   10¼" x 5⅞"

Raised   Brass   10⅜" x 5⅞"

Raised   Brass $10^{3}/_{8}$" x 6"

Raised   Cast Iron $10^{1}/_{2}$" x 6"

INVERURIE

The Locomotive Works at Inverurie were built by the Great North of Scotland Railway to replace the cramped facilities at Kittybrewster and commenced carrying out repair work in 1902. The first locomotive was constructed in 1909 and between then and 1921 a total of ten were produced. All of these were 4-4-0s. Under British Railways the workshops were converted to deal with diesel locomotives, but finally closed at the end of December 1969.

(53)

Raised   Brass $9^{3}/_{4}$" x 6"

INCHICORE

Having opened the works at Inchicore a few years earlier, the Great Southern & Western Railway produced their first locomotive in 1852 and from that time until 1957 built 404 locomotives. Of these undoubtedly the most impressive were the three Class B1A 4-6-0s (built 1939/40), which bore a striking resemblance to the LM&SR rebuilt 'Royal Scots' and the most unusual was the Bulleid designed 0-6-6-0T turf burning prototype locomotive, based on his ill-fated 'Leader' Class. This was built at Inchicore in 1957 and was scrapped sometime in late 1965 or early 1966. Diesel construction took place at the works between 1946 and 1963 during which time 40 locomotives were produced.

The GS&WR amalgamated with the Midland & Great Western Railway and the Cork, Blackrock & Passage Railway in November 1924 to form the Great Southern Railway. The following year more of the smaller railways joined the GSR to form the Great Southern Railways.

In January 1945 the GSR amalgamated with the Dublin United Transport Company to form Coras Iompair Eireann under whose jurisdiction came all road and rail transport except that belonging to the Great Northern Railway (Ireland). However, under the 1950 Transport Act CIE was nationalised and in 1958 absorbed the GNR(I) lines south of the border, which had at that time been divided between the CIE in the south and The Ulster Transport Authority in the north.

Raised   Brass   7" x $4^{1}/_{2}$"

LOCHGORM

Situated in very small premises in the triangle of lines to the east of Inverness Station, Lochgorm was renowned for its high standard of workmanship and included amongst its Locomotive Superintendents William Stroudley, David Jones and Peter Drummond, the younger brother of Dugald Drummond. Thirty-eight completely new locomotives were built between 1869 and 1906, numbered amongst which were two particularly famous types in the form of the 'Skye Bogies' and the 'Bens'. Repair work to steam locomotives finally ceased in July 1959, the site being adapted for use as a diesel facility.

Engraved   Brass $9^{7}/_{8}$" x 5"

Raised   Brass $10^{3}/_{8}$" x $5^{7}/_{8}$"

Raised   Brass $8^{3}/_{8}$" x $4^{3}/_{8}$"

KILMARNOCK

Many of the Glasgow & South Western Railway's locomotives were purchased from private builders, possibly due to the limitations of the workshops at Kilmarnock, but nevertheless between 1857 and 1921 392 new locomotives were constructed. Repairs continued to be carried out at the works until July 1959 when they were closed. Thereafter until August 1961, they acted as a store for withdrawn locomotives.

Engraved   Brass $9^{1}/_{2}$" x $5^{5}/_{8}$"

MELTON CONSTABLE

The works at Melton Constable were opened in 1883 by the Eastern & Midlands Railway and operated for a period of forty-seven years, closing in October 1930. During this time many locomotives were rebuilt but between 1897 and 1910 nine 0-6-0Ts and three 4-4-2Ts were constructed. The last of these, L&NER Class J93 No. 8489, was withdrawn in August 1949.

Raised   Brass $9^{1}/_{8}$" x $6^{1}/_{8}$"

NEASDEN

Although the Neasden Works of the Metropolitan Railway were chiefly concerned with repair and rebuilding work they did, in 1896, construct three 0-4-4Ts of Class E. A further four of this Class were built in 1900/01 but this work was undertaken by R. & W. Hawthorn Leslie & Company Limited of Newcastle upon Tyne.

| Raised | Brass | 10¾" x 5⅞" |

SWINDON

The Great Western Railway's Works at Swindon commenced operations in 1843 and became what was arguably the doyen of all the main line workshops. Locomotive construction commenced in 1846 and many famous types were produced. From the outset the locomotives designed at Swindon for the GWR had their own inimitable style and their ancestry was self-apparent. The last steam locomotive to leave the shops in 1960 was also the last to be built for British Railways. She was appropriately name 'Evening Star' and, although a Standard Class 9F 2-10-0, she was given the Swindon touch in the form of a copper-capped chimney and lined green livery. She was the 5,964th locomotive to be built there.

Diesel construction started at Swindon in 1948 and up until 1964 264 locomotives had been completed. Again Swindon continued to show its individuality by producing three classes of diesel hydraulics for main line work and one class for light freight. This endeavour was doomed, however, as British Railways decided to adopt diesel electric traction. In 1979 a rather surprising event occurred when a batch of twenty metre-gauge 0-8-0 diesel hydraulics were constructed in association with Hunslet Holdings plc for Kenya Railways. A most unusual finale for a most extraordinary works.

The amount of locomotive repair work undertaken at Swindon declined in the 1970s, but various refurbishment jobs were carried out on DMUs and EMUs. The works also became heavily involved in scrapping redundant locomotives and rolling stock. However, declining orders and British Rail's wish to rationalise working practices led to closure in March 1986.

| Raised | Brass | 12⅜" x 7⅜" |

| Raised | Brass | 12" x 7⅛" |

| Raised | Brass | 17¾" x 8¾" |

| Engraved | Brass | 5⅝" x 3¾" |

| Raised | Cast Iron | 10½" x 6" |

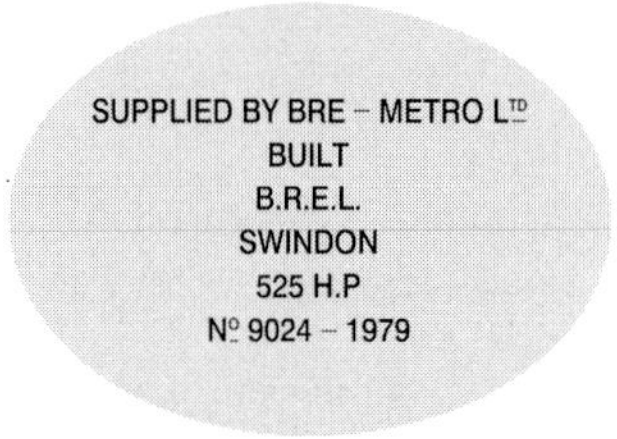

```
SUPPLIED BY BRE – METRO LTD
         BUILT
       B.R.E.L.
       SWINDON
       525 H.P
     No 9024 – 1979
```

| Raised | Brass | 11⅜" x 8" |

ST. ROLLOX

St. Rollox Works was opened in 1854 and the first locomotive, a 2-4-0, was completed in the same year. Construction continued into LM&SR days concluding with a batch of sixty LM&SR Class 4F 0-6-0s between 1924 and 1928. In total about one thousand locomotives were constructed.

Following a major reorganisation of the Scottish workshops in 1966 Cowlairs Works closed and repair work was concentrated at St. Rollox. From that time St. Rollox became known simply as Glasgow Works. In recent years repair work has been considerably reduced. In 1987 part of the works was sold to M. C. Metal Processing Limited who have scrapped many condemned British Railways diesel and electric locomotives and still operate in this capacity today.

| Raised | Brass | 10½" x 6" |

| Engraved | Brass | 8⅝" x 4⅞" |

| Engraved | Brass | 8⅝" x 4⅞" |

STOKE

For the first 20 years of its existence the North Staffordshire Railway bought from private builders, but the first locomotives built at Stoke were three small 0-6-0STs in 1868. In 1917 a single 82hp 0-4-0 battery electric locomotive was built at Stoke for use at the Oakamoor Copper Works in Staffordshire. Building continued into LM&SR days when four 0-6-2Ts were turned out during 1923. The works officially closed at the end of 1926 but in fact the run-down continued until July of the following year. It is estimated that almost two hundred locomotives were constructed at the Stoke workshops.

| Engraved | Brass | 10 1/8" x 4 3/4" |

| Raised | Brass | 10 3/8" x 6" |

| Raised | Brass | 8 5/8" x 5 5/8" |

WOLVERHAMPTON

These workshops, which were originally established by the Shrewsbury & Birmingham Railway in 1849, were situated in Stafford Road and upon absorption by the Great Western Railway in 1854 were developed to meet the ever increasing need for repair facilities. Despite cramped conditions building was also undertaken and a creditable 794 new locomotives and six steam rail motors were turned out between 1859 and 1906. The works finally closed in June 1964.

| Raised | Brass | 11 3/4" x 6" |

OTHER STANDARD LMS PLATES

(62)

| Raised | Brass | 10 1/2" x 6" |

| Raised | Brass | 10 3/8" x 5 7/8" |

| Raised | Brass | 10 3/8" x 5 7/8" |

| Raised | Brass | 10 3/8" x 5 7/8" |

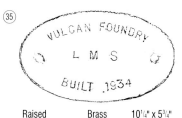

(35)

| Raised | Brass | 10 1/4" x 5 3/4" |

| Raised | Brass | 10 3/8" x 5 3/4" |

| Raised | Brass | 10 1/2" x 6" |

| Raised | Brass | 10 1/2" x 6" |

NER/LNER/BR-E
9" x 5" PLATES

These plates are listed alphabetically in workshop order

(56)

LONDON & NORTH EASTERN
RAILWAY
65855
BEYER PEACOCK & CO LTD 1908

Raised   Brass   8³/₄" x 5"

Raised   Brass   9" x 5"

(56)

Raised   Brass   9" x 5"

Raised   Brass   8⁷/₈" x 5"

Raised   Cast Iron   8⁷/₈" x 4⁷/₈"

Raised   Brass   8³/₄" x 5"

Raised   Brass   9" x 5"

(54)

Raised   Cast Iron   8⁷/₈" x 5"

Raised   Brass   8⁷/₈" x 4⁷/₈"

LONDON & NORTH EASTERN
RAILWAY
1603
REBUILT
DARLINGTON WORKS 1943

Raised   Brass   8³/₄" x 5"

Raised   Brass   9" x 5"

(55)

Raised   Brass   9" x 5¹/₈"

LONDON & NORTH EASTERN
RAILWAY
8698
DARLINGTON WORKS 1914

Raised   Brass   8³/₄" x 5"

Raised   Brass   9" x 5"

Raised   Brass   9" x 5"

Raised | Cast Iron | 9" x 5"

Raised | Brass | 9" x 5"

Raised | Brass | 9" x 5"

Raised | Brass | 9" x 5"

Raised | Brass | 8⅞" x 5"

Raised | Brass | 8⅞" x 5⅛"

Raised | Brass | 9" x 4⅞"

Raised | Brass | 8⅝" x 4¾"

Raised | Cast Iron | 9" x 5"

Raised | Cast Iron | 9" x 5"

Raised | Brass | 8¾" x 4¾"

(56)

Raised | Brass | 8⅞" x 5"

(57)

Raised | Brass | 9" x 5"

Raised | Brass | 8⅞" x 5"

Raised | Brass | 8⅝" x 4¾"

LONDON & NORTH EASTERN
RAILWAY
61933
STEPHENSON & C° 1934

Raised | Brass | 8¾" x 4¾"

Raised — Brass — 9" x 5"

⑤⑥

Raised — Cast Iron — 9" x 5"

Raised — Brass — 9" x 5"

⑤④

Raised — Brass — 9" x 5"

Raised — Brass — 8⁷/₈" x 5"

Raised — Aluminium — 9¹/₄" x 5¹/₈"

LONDON & NORTH EASTERN
RAILWAY
7461
YORKSHIRE ENG. Cº 1912

Raised — Brass — 8⁷/₈" x 4³/₄"

Raised — Brass — 8³/₄" x 5"

NOTES TO THE TEXT

1. Some plates of this pattern have number and date following contour of rim. Example – No. 1923/1927.

2. This is a replacement plate, the locomotive was rebuilt by Andrew Barclay in 1948 and was fitted with new plates of the pattern being used at that time.

3. Some plates of this pattern have number and date in straight line. Example – No. 811/1897

4. This pattern also in cast iron. Example – No. 2192/1945

5. Lettering in brackets was ground off plate. This originally read as follows:
    'THIS LOCOMOTIVE WAS COMPLETED (ON THE DAY OF GERMANY'S UNCONDITI)ON(AL SURRENDER) 7TH MAY 1945'

6. This pattern also in cast iron. Example – No. 7067/1943

7. The Robert Stephenson & Hawthorns progressive number is stamped each side of the word Darlington. '77 DARLINGTON 92'

8. Unused plate provided by builder for display purposes.

9. Plate fitted inside locomotive cab.

10. This pattern also in fibreglass. Example – No. DEL 118/1960

11. Other known horse power to this pattern. Example – 160 HP No. 2047/1934

12. Locomotive carried both Drewry Car 2169/1942 and Vulcan Foundry 4861/1942 plates.

13. Other known horse power to this pattern. Example – 153 HP No. 2588/1957

14. LONDON ground off plate.

15. Plates of this pattern dated 1965, have date in non-serif figures. Example – No 3483/E329/1965

16. Owing to the poor condition of this most interesting plate, a drawing is included to show layout of lettering. The plate was made of thin ferrous sheet and was mounted in a brass surround and glazed. It was painted white and had black lettering with grey shading.

17. This pattern also in cast iron. Example – No. 23010

18. Style of lettering varies in this pattern. Example – No. 2529/1902

19. Locomotive actually built in 1924 for Wembley Exhibition.

20. Plate bears Hudswell Clarke progressive number.

21. The rebuild plate is bolted over original building date of 1896.

22. Kerr Stuart locomotive completed by Hunslet's, but numbered in Kerr Stuart series.

23. This pattern also in brass. Example – No. 3198/1944

24. Other known cylinder sizes to this pattern, which are not illustrated, are:
    14" x 20" No. 3764/1952
    15" x 20" No. 3773/1952

25. 7103 is the original Robert Stephenson & Hawthorns' progressive number.

26. Plate is $^3/_4$" thick.

27. This pattern also in aluminium. Example – No. 1646/1937

28. Cowlairs Works replacement plate

29. This pattern also in cast iron. Example – No. 2045/1943

30. Original Robert Stephenson progressive number was 4121.

31. Original building date 1938.

32. This pattern also in cast iron. Example – No. 7086/1943

33. Darlington Works replacement plate showing locomotive running number 68024.

34. W – D = Woodhall-Duckham (the owners).

35. St. Rollox Works replacement plate.

36. The progressive number and date of build on this plate are engraved onto raised pads.

37. The Hunslet progressive number and building date is stamped onto this plate.

38. The additional plate rivetted onto the Hunslet plate has the following engraved inscription:
    'AUSTERITY LOCOMOTIVE BUILT
    FOR THE 2ND WORLD WAR
    ORIGINALLY DATED 1945
    ROBERT STEPHENSON'S NO 7204'

39. The date '1912' is stamped onto this plate, in place of the original 1909 building date, which has been ground off.

40. This pattern also in cast iron. Example – No. 1881

41. Details underlined on illustration are stamped onto plate.

42. Plate has 'REBUILT STANTON SEP 1937' stamped on bottom rim.

43. Plate has 'REBUILT STANTON 9/38' stamped on bottom rim.

44. Plate has 'NEW BOILER JULY 1912' stamped across face.

45. This plate was cast to the original L&NER pattern, by British Railways at the time of the locomotive's preservation.

46. This pattern also in fibreglass dated 1960.

47. Some plates of this pattern dated 1963 or 1964 have only two bolt holes.

48. Plate has engraved building date.

49. The number on this plate is the locomotive's running number.

50. The original 'GREAT NORTHERN RAILWAY CO' engraved inscription is filled in on this plate.

51. The original Doncaster Works progressive number and date of build have been ground off plate. The locomotive's running number is substituted.

52. This pattern also in fibreglass dated 1962.

53. The last figure of the date on this plate is engraved.

NOTES TO THE TEXT

CONTINUED

(54) The original locomotive running number on this plate was ground off and a replacement brass strip showing the 1946 renumber was substituted.

(55) Locomotive built by the North British Locomotive Co Ltd at their Atlas Works.

(56) The original locomotive running number on this plate was ground off and a replacement brass strip showing the British Railways renumber was substituted.

(57) This plate shows the Gorton Works progressive number.

(58) Other known horse powers to this pattern are:
195 HP   No.6263 – 1964
233 HP   No.6675 – 1966
252 HP   No.7187 – 1971
256 HP   No.7263 – 1972
260 HP   No.6289 – 1966
264 HP   No.5639 – 1962
311 HP   No.6294 – 1964
388 HP   No.7061 – 1971
400 HP   No.7018 – 1971
403 HP   No.7357 – 1973
562 HP   No.7401 – 1975
1124 HP   No.7288 – 1973

(59) Other known horse powers to this pattern are:
60 HP   No.4629 – 1954
102 HP   No.4263 – 1952
120 HP   No.4341 – 1952
153 HP   No.4625 – 1954
204 HP   No.4871 – 1956

(60) Other known horse powers to this pattern are:
22 HP   No.4758 – 1954
66 HP   No.6057 – 1962
70 HP   No.4101 – 1953
100 HP   No.4070 – 1958

(61) Plate bears W. G. Bagnall progressive number.

(62) A literal interpretation of the Drawing Office's instructions by the foundry resulted in a double ended arrow appearing on this plate where the builder's name should have been inserted.

(63) CEW = Central Engineering Workshops, Appleby-Frodingham Steel Co, Scunthorpe.

(64) The letters 'TD' are brazed onto this plate. It is assumed that at one time there was an 'L' preceeding these.

(65) VR = Victorian Railways, Australia.

COLLECTING
BUILDERS' PLATES

Today very few plates can be obtained from original sources and most are acquired through private deals, swap meets or auctions. Their value can vary considerably, not least because of the vagaries of the collectors' market, and while prices start at around £25, they can rise into four figures for choice examples. Bargains can, however, be found even at auction, and perhaps a general yardstick is that the older the plate and more obscure the builder the more it is likely to cost. Other factors in determining the price may also apply such as the plate's condition, where the locomotive worked, from which locomotive it was removed and the pattern of the plate.

Our publishers felt that it would be useful to give some indication of prices for those readers who are not familiar with values, but as can be appreciated from what has been said above, this was not a simple task. As there was no easy way of tackling this, a straightforward analysis of the builders' plates sold at the six Sheffield Railwayana auctions held between August 1991 and June 1992 was undertaken. These prices were still typical at the time of the book's publication. The figure shown after the builders name indicates the number of plates included in the exercise. It must be appreciated however, that they do not necessarily give a complete representation of either the upper or lower price limits for the particular builders, as, being a random sample, they do not always cover some of the more common or rarer examples. Like stocks and shares, prices may also rise or fall over a period of time.

Armstrong Whitworth	3	£100 - £420
AEI/BRCW	1	£220
W G Bagnall	2	£160 - £210
Andrew Barclay	7	£150 - £230
Beyer Peacock	10	£90 - £440
BRCW	1	£160
Drewry Car	1	£75
Dúbs	2	£400

English Electric	10	£55 - £500
John Fowler	1	£260
Grant Ritchie	1	£1100
Hawthorn Leslie	4	£180 - £260
Robert Heath	1	£1450
Hudswell Clarke	5	£35 - £215
Hunslet	2	£80 - £250
Kerr Stuart	2	£290 - £320
McCulloch Sons & Kennedy	1	£2200
McEwan Pratt	1	£360
Nasmyth Wilson	2	£580 - £1050
Neilson/Neilson Reid	4	£240 - £600
North British Locomotive	11	£95 - £440
Peckett	5	£150 - £195
Sharp Stewart	1	£390
Robert Stephenson	3	£420 - £520
Vulcan Foundry	7	£90 - £235
Yorkshire Engine, Sheffield	2	£240 - £600
Brighton, LB&SCR (engraved)	2	£500 - £620
Darlington, BR (engraved)	4	£250 - £800
Derby, BR (rectangular)	2	£30 - £40
Doncaster, GNR (engraved)	1	£610
Doncaster, LNER (engraved)	5	£400 - £600
Gorton, GCR	2	£420 - £640
Gorton, BR (engraved)	2	£300 - £340
LMS Standard ovals – various works	11	£80 - £200
LNER 9" x 5" – various works	12	£110 - £310

Replica plates are a possible difficulty for the unwary although in most cases these are honestly sold as such and are reasonably easy to distinguish from the real thing. Always obtain a vendor's name and, if in doubt, take advice. Indications that a plate is genuine include a good coat of original paint and grime, signs of scoring around bolt holes resulting from the plate being fixed to or removed from a locomotive, and rust staining on the back. Builders' plates that have been restored may have lost some of these features but some evidence is usually present. Further references to replicas can be found in *Replicas & Forgeries* published by Birmingham Railway Publications.

The authors would be only too pleased to hear from anyone who may have any builders' plates available for disposal. They would also be pleased to discuss or give advice to readers about builders' plates. Such exchanges are often of benefit to all parties, particularly if new information comes to light or existing information can be added to or corrected.

The authors may be contacted via the publishers by writing to:

Midland Publishing Limited
24 The Hollow, Earl Shilton
Leicester, LE9 7NA
England

USEFUL ADDRESSES
FOR COLLECTORS

Birmingham Railway Auctions and Birmingham Railway Publications
7 Ascot Road, Moseley, Birmingham, B13 9EN
Telephone: 0121 449 9707
Monthly collectors' magazine and monthly phone auction.

British Rail Collectors' Corner
Euston Station, London, NW1 2HS
Telephone: 0171 922 6436
The official outlet of British Rail for redundant material.
The Collectors' Corner shop is situated in Cobourg Street near Euston Station.

Charminster Collectors' Auctions
The Emporium, Mansfield Road, Parkstone, Poole, Dorset, BH12 0DD
Telephone: 01202 743 742
Regular monthly postal auctions.

Cundalls
The Cattle Market, 17 Market Place, Malton, North Yorkshire
Telephone: 01653 697 820
Auctions held regularly in Malton.

Kidlington Railwayana Auctions
58 Bloxham Road, Banbury, Oxfordshire, OX16 9JR
Telephone: 01295 251 134 or 01865 376 458
Auctions held regularly at Exeter Hall, Kidlington.

Midland Railwayana Auctions,
14 North Parade, Matlock Bath, Derbyshire, DE4 3NS
Telephone: 01629 584 085
Auctions held twice yearly at Highfields Upper School in Matlock.

Onslows
Metrostore, Townmead Road, London, SW6 2RZ
Telephone: 0171 371 0505
Auctions held regularly in London.

Quorn Swap Meet
Lavender Barn, Peveril Road, Ashby Magna, Lutterworth, Leicestershire, LE17 5NQ
Telephone: 01455 202 002 or 01162 548 301
Swap meets held three times a year (usually March, June and September) at the Great Central Railway, Quorn.

Railway Antiques Monthly
Bryn Hir, Llwyn-y-groes, Tregaron, Dyfed, SY25 6PY
Telephone: 01974 821 281
Monthly collectors' magazine and phone auction.

Railway Preservation Auctions
1 Repton Road, Brislington, Bristol, BS4 3LS
Telephone: 01179 777 458
Auctions held twice a year at Broadlands School, Keynsham, Bristol.

Sheffield Railwayana Auctions
43 Little Norton Lane, Sheffield, S8 8GA
Telephone: 01142 745 085
Quarterly auctions held at Myers Grove School, Wood Lane, Sheffield, S6 5HG.

Solent Railwayana Auctions
31 Newtown Road, Warsash, Hampshire, SO3 9FY
Telephone: 01489 578 093 or 01489 584 633
Auctions held quarterly at the Community Centre, Mill Lane, Wickham, Hampshire.

INDEX